Developing Basic Skills Programs in Secondary Schools

Daisy G. Wallace, Editor

Association for Supervision and Curriculum Development
225 N. Washington Street • Alexandria, Virginia 22314

ISBN: 0-87120-111-9
Stock No.: 611-82264
Library of Congress Card Catalog No.: 81-70310
Editing:
Ronald S. Brandt, ASCD Executive Editor
Nancy Carter Modrak, Managing Editor, Booklets

This document was produced under the provisions of the Basic Skills Improvement Office, Department of Education, Contract No. 300-80-0741. The opinions expressed do not necessarily reflect the positions, policy, or views of the Basic Skills Improvement Office or of ASCD, and no official endorsement of the Department of Education or of the Association should be inferred.

Contents

Foreword

The experienced educators contributing to this publication on the top priority concern of secondary schools have raised a number of significant questions and cited effective practices and programs.

These authors have chosen to deal with the basic skills—most commonly defined by laymen and many educators as communication and computational skills. The keys to improving the basic skills achievement of students are *involvement* and *leadership* on the part of all administrators and instructors. Each school's leadership staff needs to give consistent, visible commitment and appropriately deploy time, personnel, and instructional materials and equipment to improve achievement in the basic skills areas.

Principals cast the longest shadow of all on the quality of instructional programs by holding high expectations for student and staff performance, and by exhibiting assertive, courageous leadership in instructional concerns. In the most effective programs, staff members collaborate in establishing a system of student responsibility and direct teacher instruction using diagnosis and perscription processes; communication and feedback between teachers, students, and parents; few intrusions or distractions from instruction; and continuous staff development. Such practices as these deal with two of the major concerns in improving secondary basic skills: changing an historic pattern of student failure into success, and the lack of preparation of secondary teachers to teach the basic communication and computational skills that are normally taught at earlier levels of instruction.

In consideration of the present and future needs of a quality life for students, the definition of basic skills enlarges beyond the disciplines of reading, writing, speaking and listening, mathematics, science, the social sciences, foreign language, and the arts to include technology, literacy, analytical thinking, problem solving, and decision making. The unity of all of these competencies stems from the use of communication, thinking, and study skills, which must undergird them.

The responsibilities of the local school and school system to ensure student attainment of basic skills will be planned, implemented, and supervised by the roles represented in ASCD. The insights shared by our colleagues in this publication can assist us in building effective basic skills secondary programs. The impact of their contributions to our efforts will be evidenced in such processes as creative change approaches, the development of consistent standards and realistic policies, parental and community support, and congruency between goals and instructional outcomes.

LUCILLE G. JORDAN
President, 1981-82
Association for Supervision and
Curriculum Development

Introduction

Developing Basic Skills Programs in Secondary Schools originated as part of a two-phase project sponsored by the Basic Skills Improvement Office of the Department of Education. Under the direction of Shirley Jackson, we set out to find ways in which basic skills programs could be created and carried out at the secondary level. Traditionally, basic skills instruction has not been a major focus of junior and senior high schools, but Jackson— whose philosophy is to "do what makes sense educationally"—recognized the need to make sure that secondary level students who had not gained basic skills did so before leaving the educational system.

In the first year of this two-year project, we gathered together experts who had conducted research in the basic skills areas, and formed a national study group. These researchers, including the authors of this book, put together critical issues papers identifying what they believe to be the central concerns in developing basic skills programs at the secondary level. And, going one step further, they described what they felt principals and schools should be doing to carry out their basic skills programs. Those critical issues are what this book is all about.

The project, however, continued. In the second phase, the study group met with 150 principals from 14 Washington, D.C. area school systems. In a two-day session, the principals told the study group what *they* believe are critical issues. We at the Basic Skills Improvement Office knew that nothing the study group developed could make a significant difference if we failed to gather input from the principals themselves when trying to address their needs. As is stressed time and again in the following chapters, the principal is the single most important person in the implementation of school programs.

That brings us to the final step—answering the needs of the principals and the schools. The study group has been working on a comprehensive

vii

guide for principals to use in developing their own basic skills programs. In essence, the guide is a very precise training manual that can be used by any principal, with or without expertise in the various skills areas. When the guide is completed, we will hold five seminars around the country to train principals in its use.

Thus, *Developing Basic Skills Programs in Secondary Schools* is just one aspect of a comprehensive effort to inform principals and others not only of what should be done, but how to do it as well. This is a goal of both the Basic Skills Improvement Office and ASCD, whose members are instrumental in implementing such programs throughout the nation.

DAISY G. WALLACE
Coordinator of Secondary Basic Skills
Basic Skills Improvement Office
U.S. Department of Education

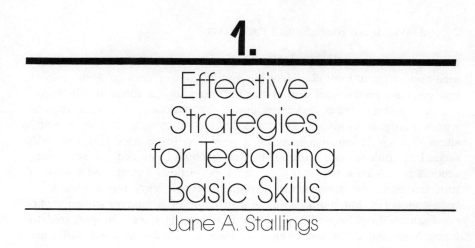

1.
Effective Strategies for Teaching Basic Skills

Jane A. Stallings

Being an educator in the 1980s is certainly challenging and sometimes overwhelming. Seldom before in the history of education have schools been confronted with such a myriad of problems—dwindling student populations, decreasing budgets, decreasing test scores, increasing parent expectations, and collective bargaining. Since most principals in schools today were trained in the 1940s, 1950s, and 1960s, little of their formal education provided methods for solving these problems. While awaiting results from current research, principals and administrators must operate with advice from friends, their own common sense, and the unforgiving school of trial and error.

Initial studies of total school programs concluded that much of the money spent to provide better libraries, laboratories, school services, and staff training did little to improve the achievement level of students.[1] In fact, to the horror of the adult population, the test scores of college-bound students plummeted to all-time lows in the 1970s. In addition, other high school students were having difficulty in mastering basic skills. High schools in the 70s inherited extensive remediation problems from the elementary schools. These problems resulted in part from the general practice in the 60s of social promotion regardless of academic achievement. This practice did not help parents of students understand the realistic consequences of not being able to read, write, and compute. Ultimately, secondary schools have borne the greatest indictment for graduating incompetent students.

[1] J. S. Coleman, E. Q. Campbell, C. J. Hobson, J. McPortland, A. M. Nood, E. D. Weinfeld, and R. L. York, *Equality of Educational Opportunity* (Washington, D.C.: Government Printing Office, 1966); R. Herrnstein, "IQ," *Atlantic Monthly* (September 1971): 43-64; C. Jencks, *Inequality: A Reassessment of the Effect of Family and Schooling in America* (New York: Basic Books, 1972); F. Mosteller and D. Moynihan, eds., *On Equality of Educational Opportunity* (New York: Vintage, 1972).

1

Parents from different sections of the country, outraged that their graduated children could not complete job applications or pass an Army test of reading, have sued school districts for not providing an adequate education.

Forty-seven states have responded by enacting laws that require students to pass minimum standards for secondary graduation. In many states this legislation also includes a provision for classes that will help secondary students gain basic skills. But teaching basic skills in secondary schools is at least a two-fold problem. First, little is known about how to turn failure into success in the secondary school. Very few studies have been conducted that could guide the instruction of secondary students who need remediation. Secondly, there are few secondary teachers prepared to teach basic skills. Because educators have assumed that basic skills are mastered in the elementary schools, secondary teacher preparation focuses on subject matter.

The purpose of this chapter is to discuss effective practices and strategies in teaching basic skills in secondary classrooms. Successful implementation of these practices is a first step toward changing patterns of student failure to patterns of success.

The education of secondary teachers has focused on subject content and curriculum. Courses or training on effective teaching strategies have been meager. In a study by Stallings and others, only 20 percent of the teachers assigned to teach basic reading skills had received training to teach reading.[2] Fortunately, in the 70s some research was funded to isolate effective strategies for helping low achieving secondary students succeed. From this work, several variables have emerged that principals and teachers should consider, including clarity in first-day organization and planning; the element of time and students on task; school policies related to effective instruction in basic skills; and staff development.

Clarity in First-Day Organization and Planning

Research by Carolyn Evertson focused on first-day organization of 102 junior high school English and mathematics classrooms.[3] Several characteristics differentiated more and less effective teacher-managers. In classrooms where there was less student misbehavior and more student achievement throughout the year:

---

[2] J. Stallings, M. Needels, and N. Stayrook, *How to Change the Process of Teaching Basic Reading Skills in Secondary Schools*. Final Report to the National Institute of Education (Menlo Park, Calif.: SRI International, 1979).

[3] C. Evertson and E. Emmer, *Effective Management at the Beginning of the School Year in Junior High Classes* (The University of Texas at Austin: Research and Development Center for Teacher Education, 1980).

1. Teachers made rules, consequences, and procedures clear on the first day. These included monitoring the students and following through with consequences for those who did not comply.

2. Teachers established a system of student responsibility and accountability for work on the first day.

3. Teachers were skillful in providing information and instruction.

4. Teachers were skillful in organizing several instructional activities.

The Element of Time and Students on Task

A study by Stallings, Cory, Fairweather, and Needels illuminated a number of instructional strategies that are effective in teaching basic skills in secondary schools.[4] These include management of class time, interactive instruction, and focus of instruction.

Management of Time

In 14 schools, the length of the class period ranged from 40 to 55 minutes. Such time differences were not related to gain in reading achievement; student learning depended on how the available time was used. In classrooms where teachers were efficient in making assignments and allocating materials, there was more time available for instruction and students made greater gains in reading. One important factor in time management is to start on time and continue until the closing bell rings. The distribution of time across several activities during the class period is also an effective strategy for keeping students on task. Effective teachers, defined as those who helped students who read at the first to fourth-grade level gain up to two grade levels in one school year, distributed time in the following way:

Activity	Percentage of Time
Instruction—giving examples, explanations, linking to student experience	16
Review and discussion of class work and story content	12
Drill and practice to help memorize	4
Oral reading in small groups	21
Silent reading	9
Written assignments	4

[4] J. Stallings, R. Cory, J. Fairweather, and M. Needels, *A Study of Basic Reading Skills Taught in Secondary Schools* (Menlo Park, Calif.: SRI International, January 1978).

The percentage of time allocated to each of these activities varied across classrooms according to student achievement levels. Interestingly, an ample amount of oral reading is helpful for low achieving students, but it is not as important for students achieving above the fourth-grade level. Oral reading activities occurred in lessons where vocabulary had been carefully developed and within small-group settings of students with similar reading skills where teachers helped students develop study concepts. Students who read below a fourth-grade level need to hear and say words as well as to read and write them. These students can usually pronounce or sound out words but often do not understand words in a story context. Secondary students' comprehension scores are often lower

**Figure 1. Distribution of Time Across Activities in
Four Ability Groups in Secondary Reading Classrooms**

Activities*	Group mean percentage of time			
	Group I	Group II	Group III	Group IV
Interactive On-Task Activities:				
Reading aloud	21%	9%	1%	1%
Instruction	16	11	17	10
Discussion	12	5	3	1
Drill and Practice	4	4	4	2
Praise/support**	19	16	7	11
Corrective feedback**	20	16	4	12
Non-Interactive On-Task Activities:				
Classroom management	12%	15%	17%	27%
Reading silently	9	16	12	21
Written assignments	4	22	23	28
Off-Task Activities:				
Social interactions	5%	6%	3%	8%
Student uninvolved	6	4	4	9

Notes: Group I—Low pretest (students at 2nd to 4th grade level)
     Gain: 4.8-5.4

     Group II—Mod pretest (students at 4th to 6th grade level)
     Gain: 5.5-7.4

     Group III—High pretest (students above 6th grade level)
     Gain: 7.8-9.5

     Group IV—No gain
     Gain 3.8-9.5

* These activities may occur simultaneously; therefore, the sum is greater than 100 percent.

** This variable is reported as frequency of observed occurrences per 45 minute period.

than their vocabulary scores. Oral reading activities allow the teacher to hear students' reading problems, ask clarifying questions, provide explanations to help students comprehend new words, and link the meaning to students' prior experience or knowledge.

Students in classrooms where slight or no gain was made spent more time than other students on written assignments (28 percent) and silent reading (21 percent). They had less instruction, discussion/review, and drill/practice. Some of these students were assigned to spend entire periods using workbooks with very little instruction from the teacher. Such classrooms often registered more student misbehavior. Students with reading problems are likely to have shorter attention spans, and the opportunity to be involved in several activities during one class period seemed to help these students keep on task.

Interactive Supportive Instruction

While studying how teachers allocated time to various classroom activities, it became clear that teachers who were interactive in their teaching style had students who achieved more in reading. This interactive style included providing oral instruction for new work, discussing and reviewing students' work, providing drill and practice, asking questions, acknowledging correct responses, and supportively correcting wrong responses.

Interactive teachers tried to include all students in classroom discussions and review sessions. The most effective teachers did not choose volunteers but rather called on particular students. When volunteers are solicited, the same people take part each day, and many students may not participate at all. When calling on a student by name, it is important to ask a question at a level on which the student is most likely to be successful. If the student gives an incorrect response, it is important that the instructor rephrase the question or give a clue so the student can succeed and give a correct answer. However, a wrong answer can provide an opportunity for the teacher to clarify and reteach, if necessary. It is important in secondary remedial classrooms to handle incorrect responses in a supportive manner, since research indicates these students do not thrive on demeaning experiences and failure.

Interactive instruction is also important when teaching subjects other than remedial reading. Good found junior high school students learned more mathematics in classrooms where teachers used active instruction.[5]

---

[5] T. L. Good, *The Missouri Mathematics Effectiveness Project* (University of Missouri at Columbia: School of Education, 1980).

These teachers made assignments and provided information in a clear manner. They asked students appropriate questions and provided immediate feedback to student responses. Unfortunately, many teachers of general mathematics students are not active in their teaching style. In a study of mathematics classes in 11 schools, Stallings and Robertson found that teachers more often used written workbook assignments and less often reviewed class work or directly instructed students in general mathematics classes than did teachers in geometry or calculus classes.[6] In classrooms where students are more involved, more achievement occurs. Students in general mathematics or pre-algebra classes were off-task significantly more often than were students in algebra II, geometry, or calculus classes.

**Figure 2. Percentage of Student Time Spent in
Activities for Three Types of Mathematics Classes***

Variables	Type I	Type II	Type III
Instruction	14.0%	25.0%	30.0%
Review	8.0	21.0	23.0
Written Assignments	34.0	15.0	11.0
Teacher Management (no students)	24.0	20.0	15.0
Social Interactions	11.0	13.0	13.0
Students Uninvolved	11.0	6.0	4.0
Discipline	4.0	0.20	0.05

Type I: General math or Pre-Algebra
Type II: Algebra I, Geometry
Type III: Algebra II, Trigonometry, Calculus
* Because some categories overlap, columns do not sum to 100%.

Eleven teachers in the study were observed in both lower and advanced mathematics classes. When observations of the teachers were compared, researchers found the same teacher would be active with advanced classes and *not* with lower mathematics classes. These low-achieving students need instruction from teachers to stay on task. Programmed workbooks do not help them learn the mathematical relationships necessary to cope with life. A teacher can see understanding in students' faces; when understanding is not apparent, a teacher can select another example from the students' backgrounds and explain it on the chalkboard.

---

[6] J. Stallings and A. Robertson, *Factors Influencing Women's Decisions to Enroll in Elective Mathematics Classes in High School*. Final Report to the National Institute of Education (Menlo Park, Calif.: SRI International, 1979).

The most important research finding is that teachers need to *actively* teach. Note: relationships similar to those described in mathematics classes were also found in general science and physics classes. The advanced classes received active instruction and the less able students in general science classes received workbook assignments. This is not effective instruction for low achieving students.

Focus of Instruction

If teachers use an interactive instructional style, to whom should they focus their instruction—individuals, small groups, or the total group? During the last decade, considerable energy has been directed toward the development of individualized programs. Federal, state, and local funds have been spent to develop programmed reading, mathematics, and science books. All of these programmed materials were directed to giving children activities through which they could progress at their own rates. It was assumed that if students worked at their own pace through a series of seqential exercises, learning would occur. It did for some students, but it did not for others. In general, there has been a great disillusionment with individualized instruction. Some students learn best when new information is presented to a small group of students who are operating at a similiar pace.[7] Learning occurs when students read aloud, hear others read aloud, and hear others ask questions and respond. Hearing and speaking as well as reading and writing help students integrate and retain information. Individualized programs based almost totally on workbooks do not allow for this type of group learning.

At a conference on instructional dimensions sponsored by the National Institute of Education, 60 teachers discussed their experiences and attitudes toward individualized instruction. Teachers reported that in most individualized programs they felt their role was relegated to record keeping. When workbooks were relied on to provide student instruction, teachers felt unable to integrate the students' learning.[8] It appears that students need interactions with teachers. A teacher can develop concepts with a group and change examples or illustrations to coincide with the group's background experience. If students do not understand, the teacher can find yet

---

[7] J. Stallings, "Implementation and Child Effects of Teaching Practices in Follow Through Classrooms," *Monographs of the Society for Research in Child Development* (December 1975): 50-93.

[8] M. Amarel and J. Stallings, "Individualized Instruction," in *Perspectives on the Instructional Dimension Study* (Washington, D.C.: National Institute of Education, 1978).

another example. Books or machines don't do that. They provide opportunities to practice and reinforce instruction, but research suggests that by themselves, books or machines are not sufficient to provide the instruction students need. Supervisors and principals can support well-focused instruction, interactive teaching, and effective time management by making teachers aware of research findings and providing appropriate inservice training.

School Policies Related to Effective Basic Skills Instruction

Student outcomes are related to effective classroom practices, which may be dependent on school practices and policies. Rutter found that secondary student achievement, attendance, and delinquency were related to several school variables:

- Consistent expectations for students throughout school; for example, coming to class on time.
- An emphasis on pupil success and potential; for example, monthly awards for achievement, attendance, sports, drama, and music.
- Clear, direct, and timely communication and feedback to teachers and students.
- Teacher willingness to see students for personal assistance.
- Joint curriculum planning by staff.
- Good school repair and maintenance (students encouraged to respect surroundings and behave appropriately).[9]

While working with teachers to change specific behaviors, Stallings, Needels, and Stayrook found several school policy variables that were related to student achievement.[10] They included policies toward absences, cuts, and tardiness; instruction; assignment of teachers to classrooms; assignment of students to classrooms; grading systems; availability of student information; reading in the content area; and parental support. All of these variables can be manipulated to some degree by teachers and principals.

Absence Rate and Tardiness

Responses from a sample of San Francisco Bay Area secondary principals reveal that student absences contribute significantly to the problem of low achievement. In this sample, the absence rate (which included cuts)

---

[9] M. Rutter, B. Maughan, P. Mortimer, and J. Ouston, *Fifteen Thousand Hours* (Cambridge, Mass.: Harvard University Press, 1979).

[10] Stallings, Needels, and Stayrook, 1979.

ranged from 5 to 25 percent. This rate is higher for low achieving students. Clearly, teachers cannot reach students who do not appear in class. However, there is a relationship between student absences and teacher instructional style. In our study of teaching strategies in secondary remedial reading classrooms, we found that students were absent *less* often in classrooms where the following variables existed to a greater degree:

- Students perceived the classroom to be a friendly place.
- Students perceived some competitiveness and high expectations.
- Teachers provided ample verbal instruction.
- Teachers provided instruction to the total class.
- Students sometimes were leaders and provided information to the class—oral reports and the like.
- Students had opportunities to read aloud.

Students were absent significantly *more* often in classrooms where the following variables existed to a greater degree:

- Students spent the majority of class time doing written assignments in workbooks.
- Students spent the majority of class time reading silently.
- Teachers did management tasks—grading papers, making lesson plans, and keeping records—and were not involved with students during the majority of class time.
- Students were being disciplined for disruptive behavior.

Absence rates and tardiness need to be brought under control at the school level as well as at the classroom level. Following are some techniques used successfully by schools:

- Call at night (between 7 and 9 p.m.) to report absent or tardy students. In many families both parents work. Night calls require volunteers or payment for someone to call consistently. One school with a 25 percent absentee rate reduced it to 12 percent within a one-month period.
- The clergy in one school district volunteered two hours each morning. They greeted tardy students and called parents at home or at work to report tardy or absent students. This school reduced its absentee rate from 40 percent to 15 percent within the school year.
- Students who cut class or were tardy accumulated time to be used assisting the school custodian in cleaning the grounds and lavatories at lunch time, after school, or on Saturday mornings. This school's absence rate dropped from 15 percent to 9 percent.

To reduce absenteeism and tardiness, it is necessary to have a *state school policy* that details all of the penalties for noncompliance clearly to students, parents, and staff. *Consistency* of consequences for noncompliance is the key to reducing illegal cuts and tardiness. If some personnel follow school policy and others do not, students will concentrate on trying to find where the rules can be bent. Sometimes principals must reprimand a teacher or staff member for being too lax with students and unsupportive of school policy. Clarity and consistency seem to be the key to solving attendance problems.

Intrusions

Research by Stallings, Needels, and Stayrook indicates that in classrooms with more intrusions from the outside (announcements on the intercom, requests for students to leave the room, tardy entrances by students) students make less gain in basic reading skills.[11] Other school personnel (counselors, school paper editors, drama coaches, physical education coaches, music directors, detention officers) may not appreciate how difficult it is to get a classroom of low ability students *on task* and productive, and how easy it is for them to get *off task*. When interruptions are allowed during class time, students may infer that what is occurring in the classroom lacks value.

School administrators can establish clear guidelines about the sacrosanct nature of classroom teaching; if we are serious about teaching basic skills, no one disturbs a teacher when class is in session. Nothing less than a cataclysmic event should stop a teaching session. Some administrators allow 10 minutes for announcements at the beginning of the day rather than making random announcements. One classroom in our study had 20 intrusions during a 45-minute period. Clearly, it is difficult to accomplish academic tasks in such an environment.

Assignment of Classrooms to Teachers

Research also indicates that remedial reading students gain more when teachers have permanent classrooms. Basic skills teachers need to arrange a reading environment where student growth charts can be displayed so that students can keep track of their progress. Teachers need diagnostic and prescriptive materials, and many high interest books at the right reading level at their fingertips. Teachers who must shift from one classroom to another cannot create an environment conducive to developing basic reading skills.

---

[11] Stallings, Needels, and Stayrook, 1979.

Classrooms should be large so that students can be arranged in groups whenever small-group instruction is needed. As indicated earlier, small-group instruction is beneficial to secondary students who read at or below the fourth-grade level.

Assignment of Students to Classrooms

Students who require remediation make more progress in homogeneously grouped classrooms. Gains made by low achieving students have been related to class size and achievement level. Students below a fourth-grade level gained more when the class size averaged 18 students. Students between fourth and sixth-grade achievement level made gains in classes averaging 21 students, and students above the sixth-grade achievement level made gains in classes averaging 26 students. Teachers more often used written workbook assignments and less often reviewed class work or directly instructed in classes with general mathematics students than in geometry or calculus classes. These data suggest that students who achieve at a lower level should be placed in smaller classes than students who achieve at a higher level.

A classroom of 40 students with one or more teacher aides is not a good situation for the remedial student. These students tend to be easily distracted and the more bodies there are, the more distractions there are to filter.

These data do not advocate tracking or laning, but they do suggest that smaller classes and some homogenous grouping are effective for basic skills classes.

Grading Systems

Remedial classes need a variable grading system. Students who have a history of failure thrive best when they can experience daily success in programs that provide daily gains and 80 percent to 100 percent achievement scores on exercises. Remedial students will be overwhelmed with a sense of failure if they still receive a D or F on their report cards because their achievement is below grade level. Some teachers try to console their students by saying that a 90 percent F is not as bad as a 30 percent F. However, any F means failure to students and parents and may discourage students from further effort. In view of this, several possible alternative procedures are proposed:

• Identify the class as a basic skills course for improvement in reading, and assign grades on the basis of a student's progress in the course.

For example, a tenth-grade student who tested at a second-grade reading level when the course began and progressed to a fifth-grade reading level made excellent progress. This student should receive an A for improvement even though his or her reading achievement is still below grade level.

• Variable credit could be earned on productivity. In a five-credit course, students who complete half of the work in one semester might receive two and a half credits of C work rather than failing and receiving no credit. Some students learn more slowly than others, but they can and do learn if given adequate time. "Faster is not necessarily better." [12]

• In schools where the previous two suggestions are not acceptable, E, S, or N might be used to indicate that excellent, satisfactory, or no progress has been made.

Changing from one grading system to another is a difficult task that requires parental support as well as school staff support. Schools should allow a year to plan and consult with other schools using variable grading systems.

Student Information

Although teachers need information about students' reading problems and reading levels at the time classes are assigned, most teachers surveyed did not have student information readily available. Teachers feel their ability to select materials to match student needs would increase if at least the reading levels of students were printed on the class lists.

To obtain reading scores, teachers must go through counselors' files and record the data available for each of the 100 to 150 students in their classes. This requires 5 to 10 minutes per student. After searching the records, they may find that test information is not available for many students. Testing programs are particularly lax in many secondary schools; test data are often several years old; and transfer student records may not be available until the middle or end of the semester.

In the past, there was a reluctance to make test scores easily available to teachers for fear that this information might prejudice teachers' attitudes toward students. However accurate this reluctance might be for other subject areas, it should not apply to basic reading skills teachers, who need all of the information that is available. While reading level is not by itself sufficient information, it will help teachers understand the range of student abilities. Basic skills teachers need more student information since sec-

---

[12] Benjamin Bloom, *Human Characteristics and School Learning* (New York: McGraw-Hill Book Company, 1967).

ondary students who have a history of failure in reading are likely to have some perceptual, physical, or emotional problems in addition to reading problems of encoding, decoding, and comprehension. Group tests such as those developed by the Cincinnati School District gather these types of student information.

In addition to providing student information to secondary teachers of reading, a strong case can be made for providing inservice workshops on how to diagnose reading problems and prescribe corrective treatment. Workshops on the use of diagnostic and prescriptive materials should be conducted in the summer so that teachers can diagnose student problems during the first week of school. In some school districts, students start school several days after teachers report in the fall. Students who need remediation are scheduled for diagnostic testing during teacher preparation days, and teachers select appropriate programs for students before school begins.

Reading in the Content Area

Teachers who must try to teach reading in the content area need textbooks that provide similar information at different reading levels. Most often such materials are not available. In that case several options are available:

• Teachers may attempt to write their own materials for students with low reading ability. Several teachers could share this responsibility.

• Teachers may try to locate or develop audio tapes of textbooks (states produce some of these for use with the blind).

• Teachers may develop detailed teaching frameworks so that students can comprehend key concepts.

In any case, the administrative staff should convene interdepartmental meetings to discuss and clarify the policy regarding reading in the content area. If this topic is not addressed, many able students with poor reading skills may be penalized unfairly in social studies, science, and mathematics.

Parental Support

Administrators can create an atmosphere in which parents feel needed to help in their child's education—not only to work on school committees, but also to help their child learn required skills. Some skills simply need more drill or practice, and some ideas may need discussion.

Research on the effect of parents' school involvement on children's progress reports a positive relationship under the following conditions:

• Parents are given specific tasks to do with the children. For example, they receive materials and directions for helping children at home.[13]

• School personnel provide parents with training as well as with materials.[14]

Administrators can develop a policy that guides teachers to elicit positive, active support from parents for their child's education. If teachers see parents as a source of energy to help children learn, shared efforts can lighten the teaching burden. It is important that parents and teachers feel they are striving together toward a common goal: to help the student learn necessary skills. Since there are currently large numbers of families with a single working parent or two working parents, some schools have arranged for evening meetings with parents to encourage joint efforts. In this arrangement, counselors or teachers may be given school-day release time.

Staff Development

In the past, dollar support for staff development has not been a problem. The problem has been in delivering a well-focused, comprehensive program that serves both student and teacher needs. In a study of 20 Teacher Corps sites, it appeared that there was little coordination among categorical programs. Seldom did personnel from Teacher Centers, Teacher Corps, or other categorical aid programs jointly plan projects for teachers and students. Teachers in the study schools reported that the activities of several federal programs in a school seem to fragment children's education. Also, when there are several staff development programs in a school, they often compete for teachers' limited time. If each categorical program has a director and its own budget, the program becomes the focus rather than children and teachers. Isolated pull-out programs seem to work to the disadvantage of children. In schools where the administrator appoints one person to coordinate several programs, joint planning to meet children's needs and teachers' training needs is more likely to occur. In the face of dwindling dollars, schools more than ever need a well-focused, comprehensive staff development program.

---

[13] L. Corno, *Effects of Parent Instruction on Teacher Structuring and Student Participation in the Third Grade: An Aptitude-Treatment Interaction Approach* (Stanford, Calif.: Stanford University, May 1978).

[14] I. J. Gordon, *Early Child Stimulation Through Parent Education*. Final Report to the U.S. Children's Bureau (Gainesville, Fla.: College of Education, University of Florida, 1969).

Choosing A Staff Development Program

Many districts have a budget for staff development. The budget supports a given number of days for teacher release time, attendance at professional conferences, or inservice consultants. During the past four years of studying schools, we have found that principals use these funds in very different ways. For example, some principals allow each staff member to attend two conferences out of a list of several that are deemed acceptable. It is important to follow-up and see how the teachers benefited from the conference. If there is no follow-up, teachers will not have the opportunity to share what they learned with their colleagues.

Some principals use their funds to establish a schoolwide program for training a group of teachers in specific techniques. Those teachers then become trainers for the entire staff.[15] Other programs train a total school or district staff.[16]

Staff development seems most effective in changing teacher behavior and student achievement when the program is schoolwide. For instance, one school requires every teacher to teach the meaning and spelling of at least five key words a week. These words must be central to a course of study. Misspellings are handled the same way in every class. Over a two-year period, this school significantly increased student spelling and vocabulary scores on a standardized test.

A Model For Staff Development

Every staff development model includes a curriculum and a delivery system. Curriculum is the content, and delivery is the where, when, how, and number of participants. A good curriculum with poor delivery, or vice versa, is not likely to be effective in changing teacher behavior.

The goal of one such staff development model is to help teachers learn to manage classroom time effectively.[17] The curriculum is based on research findings, and the delivery system offers personalized instruction and interactive, small-group problem solving. The content of the model

---

[15] *Assertive Discipline,* conducted by Lee Cantor, Fremont, California; and *Classroom Management Training Program,* conducted by Frederick Jones, Santa Cruz, California.

[16] *Increasing Teaching Effectiveness,* a four-part workshop series conducted by Madeline Hunter, Los Angeles; and *Equal Opportunity in the Classroom,* now called *Teachers' Expectations and Student Achievement* (TESA), conducted by Sam Kerman, Los Angeles County Department of Education.

[17] *The Teaching and Learning Institute,* directed by Jane Stallings, Mountain View, California.

derives from research funded by the National Institute of Education, which also provided funds for developing the delivery system.[18]

Development of the model occurred during a multi-phase study in secondary schools. In Phase I, researchers selected and observed 45 secondary reading classrooms from six northern California school districts to examine the relationship between what teachers do and what students gain in reading. Study results provided some very specific guidelines on efficient instructional strategies to use with secondary remedial reading students. In Phase II, researchers translated these findings into a series of workshops and trained 47 teachers in the Phase I districts and one neighboring district. Half of the teachers were in a training group, and the other half were in a control group that did not receive training until the end of the experiment. The treatment teachers changed behaviors in recommended ways, and their students made greater gains in reading achievement than did the students in the control group. The teachers were enthusiastic about the program and recommended the training to other teachers in their districts. To accommodate requests that were beyond the scope of our staff, we developed a Phase III program, which monitored our trained teachers as they trained other teachers in their districts. Through this three-phase effort, the districts acquired a cadre of teacher trainers, a staff development model, and effective instructional methods for helping students gain basic reading skills.

As noted earlier, students made more achievement gain in classrooms where teachers spent more time instructing, discussing homework, providing considerable supportive feedback, and using oral reading by students in small groups. In this environment, the teacher stayed involved with students throughout the class period. Teachers were well organized and used the available time effectively.

Students made less achievement gain in classrooms where 40 to 50 percent of class time was allocated to written assignments, another 30 to 40 percent was allocated to silent reading, and the remainder was spent grading papers, making lesson plans, and handling social or disruptive interactions. These classrooms did not provide the supportive interaction that remedial students need to make progress. To optimize student gain, these findings suggest that teachers should "get the show on the road" when the bell rings and stay supportively involved during the total class period.

---

[18] The early research was carried out at SRI International in Menlo Park, California.

The following is a list of variables found to be significantly related ($p < .05$) to reading achievement gain:

Positively Related	Negatively Related
Discussing or reviewing classwork or homework	Teachers doing organization or management tasks during class time
Instructing new work	Too much time allocated to written assignment
Students reading aloud	
Focusing instruction on a small group or the total group	Too much time allocated to working with one student
Positive corrective feedback for incorrect responses (rephrased probing or questions)	Intrusions (loudspeakers, tardy students)
	Uninvolved students and social interactions
Short quizzes	Misbehavior or negative interactions

The goal of Phase II was to change teacher behavior in specific ways. A treatment group and a control group of teachers were observed in the fall, winter, and spring. Only the treatment teachers participated in the five workshops based on research findings from Phase I. Each treatment teacher received a profile of his or her own behavior developed from objective observations in the classroom. A set of specific recommendations were made to each teacher to increase or decrease certain behaviors. The workshops provided assistance on these changes.

Workshop sessions were conducted one week apart—usually from 3:30 to 6:00 p.m. To maximize interactions and full participation, groups were limited to five or six teachers. Although workshop materials were used, the cornerstone of the workshops was encouragement to try new ideas for change. Each teacher operated in a unique situation. Class size, room assignment, and school policies affected the way recommendations were implemented. The trainer listened to teachers' questions and ideas about the research and encouraged teachers to help each other seek solutions to specific problems. All recommendations were examined and adjusted to individual situations of teachers, students, classrooms, and schools.

At the end of the semester, teachers were observed again and behavior change was measured. For the most part, treatment teachers changed behavior according to the midwinter recommendations. A late spring observation indicated that treatment teachers maintained most of their behavior changes. In contrast, control teachers' classes became more lax and less task-oriented. More importantly, the treatment teachers' students made greater reading achievement gains.

Principals can develop a similar model by (1) observing teachers or having teachers observe each other, (2) providing some staff development program, and (3) observing again at the end of the program. It is important to observe and document teaching behavior to be changed by the intervention, so that teachers can be given specific feedback on their behaviors.

Summary

Some of the most important points to emerge from research on effective schooling for students who must gain basic skills are:

• Teachers need to be interactive and directly involved with students to keep them on task.

• Teachers should distribute questions to all members of the class and be supportive and guiding in their feedback.

• Teachers should offer several activities during a class period so that students can develop listening, speaking, reading, and writing skills. This helps students integrate information.

• Teachers need a well-focused, comprehensive, continuous staff development program to gain the skills needed to be effective teachers.

• Schools should allow minimal distractions to intrude on classroom time.

• Schools should have a consistent and enforced policy for absences, tardiness, and misbehavior.

• Schools should seek parental participation and support.

• Effective schools are a friendly place to be—teachers are available to students, schools are kept in good repair, student success is recognized throughout the school.[19]

Teachers need help to effectively teach the students in their classrooms. The onus is upon the school administrative staff to select a training curriculum that is focused on school improvement. Further, the program should be comprehensive and continuous, with opportunities for teachers to receive feedback on their progress. Every program should be evaluated for effectiveness by observing teacher behavior before and after the intervention and then measuring teacher change. The impact on student achievement and absence rates should then be evaluated. The bulwark of public education is being challenged, and it is imperative that the teachers in our schools be prepared to meet that challenge.

---

[19] M. Rutter, B. Maugham, P. Mortimore, and J. Ouston, *Fifteen Thousand Hours* (Cambridge, Mass.: Harvard University Press, 1979).

References

Amarel, M., and Stallings, J. "Individual Instruction." In *Perspectives on the Instructional Dimension Study*. Washington, D.C.: National Institute of Education, 1978.

Bloom, B. *Human Characteristics and School Learning*. New York: McGraw-Hill Book Company, 1976.

Coleman, J. S.; Campbell, E. Q.; Hobson, C. J.; McPortland, J.; Nood, A. M.; Weinfeld, E. D.; and York, R. L. *Equality of Educational Opportunity*. Washington, D.C.: Government Printing Office, 1966.

Corno, L. *Effects of Parent Instruction on Teacher Structuring and Student Participation in the Third Grade: An Aptitude-Treatment Interaction Approach*. Stanford, Calif.: Stanford University, May, 1978.

Evertson, C., and Emmer, E. *Effective Management at the Beginning of the School Year in Junior High Classes*. Austin, Tx.: Research and Development Center for Teacher Education, University of Texas, 1980.

Gordon, I. J. *Early Child Stimulation Through Parent Education*. Final report to the U.S. Children's Bureau. Gainesville, Fla.: College of Education, University of Florida, 1969.

Good, T. L. *The Missouri Mathematics Effectiveness Project*. Columbia, Mo.: School of Education, University of Missouri, 1980.

Jencks, C. *Inequality, A Reassessment of the Effect of Family and Schooling in America*. New York: Basic Books, 1972.

Mosteller, F., and Moynihan, D., eds. *On Equality of Educational Opportunity*. New York: Vintage, 1972.

Herrnstein, R. "IQ." *Atlantic Monthly* 228 (September 1972): 43-64.

Rutter, M.; Maughan, B.; Mortimore, P.; and Ouston, M. J. *Fifteen Thousand Hours*. Cambridge, Mass.: Harvard University Press, 1979.

Stallings, J. "Implementation and Child Effects of Teaching Practices in Follow Through Classrooms." *Monographs of the Society for Research in Child Development* 40 (December 1975): 50-93.

Stallings, J.; Cory, R.; Fairweather, J.; and Needels, M. *A Study of Basic Reading Skills Taught in Secondary Schools*. Menlo Park, Calif.: SRI International, January 1978.

Stallings, J.; Needels, M.; and Stayrook, N. *How to Change the Process of Teaching Basic Reading Skills in Secondary Schools*. Final report to the National Institute of Education. Menlo Park, Calif.: SRI International, 1979.

Stallings, J., and Robertson, A. *Factors Influencing Women's Decisions to Enroll in Elective Mathematics Classes in High School*. Final report to the National Institute of Education. Menlo Park, Calif.: SRI International, 1979.

2.

Language

Arnulfo G. Ramirez

Language is the common denominator of basic skills, which are defined as oral and written communication skills, reading comprehension, and competence in mathematics. Language is also the principal means by which teaching and learning activities are conducted. Teachers and pupils talk, listen, read, and write as they participate in the educational process. Teaching and learning typically comprise such linguistic activities as questioning, explaining, discussing, answering, listening, repeating, paraphrasing, and synthesizing. Language is central to basic skills and the transmission of subject matter.

Language Use in the Basic Skills

Basic skills involve, in part, the learning of specialized vocabularies to discuss subject matter. Students need to understand such terms as *word, sound, letter, sentence,* and *paragraph* in order to participate effectively in reading lessons. To discuss or solve mathematics problems, a conceptual knowledge of terms like *sum, invert, subtract, coefficient,* and *right-angled triangle* is also essential. To extend students' abilities to use language for different oral and written communicative purposes, explicit instruction, demonstration, and practice are required. Using language appropriately for social situations involves knowing *how* to say *what* (beat it, you better go now, would you please leave), to *whom* (kid brother, friend, stranger), *when* (after an argument, after a date, before being introduced), and *where* (backyard, library). This may mean performing the following major communication functions.

1. *Controlling*—These are communication acts in which the participant's dominant function is to control behavior, for example, commanding, offering, suggesting, permitting, threatening, warning, prohibiting, contracting, refusing, bargaining, rejecting, acknowledging, justifying, persuading, and arguing.

20

2. *Feeling*—These are communication acts which express and respond to feelings and attitudes, such as exclaiming, expressing a state or an attitude, taunting, commiserating, tale-telling, blaming, disagreeing, and rejecting.

3. *Informing*—These are communication acts in which the participant's function is to offer or seek information, for example, stating information, questioning, answering, justifying, naming, pointing out an object, demonstrating, explaining, and acknowledging.

4. *Ritualizing*—These are communication acts which serve primarily to maintain social relationships and to facilitate social interaction, such as greeting, taking leave, participating in verbal games, (pat-a-cake), reciting, taking turns in conversations, participating in culturally appropriate speech modes (for example, teasing, shocking, punning, praying, playing the dozens), and demonstrating culturally appropriate amenities.

5. *Imagining*—These are communication acts which cast the participants in imaginary situations and include creative behaviors such as role playing, fantasizing, speculating, dramatizing, theorizing, and storytelling.[1]

These communication functions also apply when the student learns to write. The student may learn to eliminate the use of colloquialisms (*we have none* for *we don't have any*) and nonstandard forms (*ain't, he going*) when using formal, written English. As with oral communication, writing is used for different purposes and audiences (personal letter to a friend, sharing information or persuading a stranger, and creating stories and poems for classmates). The range of language use in the "different" basic skills may vary, but for the individual student, it requires different forms based on a common underlying competency in major communication functions.

Language and the Curriculum

Language enters into the curriculum in two ways: (1) as a *system of communication* (teachers explaining a lesson or telling students what to do, students asking questions); and (2) as a *means of learning* (students discussing the meaning of a story or writing answers to questions after reading a chapter from the history text).

Language is both *process* and *product*. In an English class, for instance, the desired product may be a persuasive essay on "Why Women Should/Shouldn't Be Drafted." The process may involve reading magazine articles or discussing the issues in small groups. In a history class, the teacher's explanation or lecture (oral language) is the process used to trans-

---

[1] Barbara Sundene Wood, *Development of Functional Communication Competencies: Grades 7-12* (Urbana, Ill.: ERIC Clearinghouse on Reading and Communication Skills, 1977), pp. 2-5.

mit knowledge about the American Revolution. A student's written description of a laboratory experiment in chemistry is a process that produces a product through which the teacher can assess the student's understanding of scientific phenomena.

Talking, listening, reading, and writing—four modalities of language —are often interrelated in the process of teaching, but they are not equally developed. Recent research efforts in Britain suggest that all four language modes should be developed.

The influential Bullock Report, *A Language for Life,* made a number of recommendations regarding language and learning competence growth and the need to develop a general language policy to help teachers understand the relationship between language and thought:

Language competence grows incrementally through an interaction of writing, talking, reading, and experience, and the best teaching deliberately influences the nature and quality of this growth.

Language has a unique role in developing human learning: the higher processes of thinking are normally achieved by the interaction of a child's language behaviour with his other mental and perceptual powers.

A stimulating classroom environment will not necessarily of itself develop the children's ability to use language as an instrument for learning. The teacher has a vital part to play, and his role should be one of planned intervention.

Competence in language comes above all through its purposeful use, not through the working of exercises divorced from context.[2]

Determining the Uses of Language Across the Curriculum

Language uses—making oral reports, taking notes, reading textbooks —affect both the degree of student involvement, passive versus active participation, and the development of particular oral/written communicative abilities. In one sense, "every teacher is a language teacher," and "every lesson is a language lesson." The biology teacher cannot separate the teaching of concepts and facts about biology from the teaching of the specialized language of biology and its uses. This interrelationship is best illustrated by examples of student explanations. The best scientific description of an earthworm is also the most developed in its use of language.

1. It is long and thin. It is brown in colour. It has rings around it. It has no eyes. It is slimy.

2. It is long and thin and brown. It has segments along its body. It has

---

[2] *A Language for Life* (London: Her Majesty's Stationery Office, 1975).

a black patch on it called the saddle. Its skin has rough patches underneath. It is slimy.

3. The earthworm has a body shaped like a closed tube made up of segments or rings which help to make it flexible. The mouth of the animal is at the pointed end—the anus at the flattened end. There is a blood vessel running down the dorsal surface of the animal and visible through the skin. Approximately one-third of the body length from the mouth end is the saddle, which is unsegmented. All the body is moist to the touch.[3]

Various procedures can be used to determine specific uses of the four language modalities. These include the use of classroom observations, oral interviews, and written questionnaires. A written survey with a checklist format can represent a graphic profile by department (English, science, reading) and grade (ninth, tenth, eleventh). A profile can clearly identify a school's language policy. The survey of *Linguistic Demands in the Classroom,* developed in 1979 by Ramirez and Bayer as part of a Teacher Corps Project at Stanford University/San Jose Unified School District, is presented on page 26. This instrument examines both the *frequency* and *purpose* of various linguistic activities.

Changing School Language Policy

Changing the uses of language across the curriculum cannot be done in isolation from other considerations. Keen has suggested a framework for examining the uses of language and ways of thinking about languages for educational purposes.[4] Using language includes four areas:

1. *Demands:* What demands are made on students' language resources (e.g., in different subject areas and grade levels)?

2. *Resources:* What resources do students have to meet these demands (e.g., writing abilities, reading competencies)?

3. *Problems:* Under what circumstances are the resources adequate or inadequate for the demands made?

4. *Solutions:* What can be done to bridge gaps between resources and demands (e.g., altering ways of teaching/testing; uses of language)?

Thinking about language explores students' linguistic awareness in terms of theory and reality:

1. *Theory:* What theories and ideas about language do students already have?

---

[3] Jill Richards, *Classroom Language: What Sort?* (London: George Allen and Unwin, 1978).

[4] John Keen, *Teaching English, A Linguistic Approach* (London: Methuen and Co., Ltd., 1978), pp. 109-111.

2. *Reality:* How do these theories match the way students use language?

While this framework may appear ambitious, it does include students' linguistic awareness, which should be developed. Marland argues that the ultimate aim of a "language across the curriculum policy" is to create a "virtuous circle":

[I]f a school devotes thought and time to assisting language development, learning in all areas will be helped; if attention is given to language in the content and skill subjects, language development will be assisted powerfully by the context and purpose of those subjects.[5]

School language policy cannot be changed without influencing teachers' knowledge and attitudes about language. To influence teachers, the San Jose (California) High School used a series of workshops with guest speakers and specific objectives for the participants. In Woodberry (England) Lower School, a group of teachers formed a "working party" to develop specific guidelines for language policy. In any case, five basic steps are involved in language policy development:

1. *Assessment of language demands*—conducting a survey, interviewing teachers, meetings by subject area.

2. *Interpretation of assessment results*—arranging small discussions, holding workshops, establishing a language policy committee.

3. *Formulation of a language policy*—developing different uses of language for the teaching/learning process based on recommendations from the language policy committee; making specific changes within individual departments.

4. *Implementation of new language policy*—changing instructional approaches or the uses of reading and writing on assignments/testing.

5. *Reformulation of the language policy*—examining pupil reactions, interviewing teachers, holding departmental meetings. [See page 29 for a questionnaire developed by secondary science teachers in England to assess pupils' attitudes toward the contexts (teacher-pupil, pupil-pupil) and uses of language (asking questions, completing charts).]

The Bullock Report from England argues that a comprehensive school language policy and teacher awareness about the educational functions of language are needed.

Each school should have an organized policy for language across the curriculum, establishing every teacher's involvement in language and reading development throughout every school year.

---

[5] Michael Marland, ed., *Language Across the Curriculum* (London: Heinemann Educational Books, 1977), p. 3.

Every LEA (local education agency) should appoint a special English advisor and should establish an advisory team with the specific responsibility of supporting schools in all aspects of language in education.

A substantial course on language in education (including reading) should be a part of every primary and secondary school teacher's initial training, whatever the teacher's subject or the age of the children with whom he or she will be working.

The Effect of School Language Policy on Instructional Approaches

Instructional approaches used in secondary schools make specific linguistic demands on pupils. Participants in the conversation (teacher-pupil and pupil-pupil) and the nature of the classroom group (students in a small group, teacher-to-individual pupil, and teacher-to-whole class) affect the type of language (informal or formal) and thought-ordering activities (implicit and explicit) demanded of students. Normal classroom activities allow for teacher-pupil interaction but usually do not encourage active pupil-pupil dialogue related to the lesson. A pupil-to-pupil dialogue, conducted in small groups, allows students to order knowledge through informal language (exploratory talk) before presenting knowledge (interpretation of the story or article, description of a scientific process, solution to a mathematics problem) to the whole class for public (formal) discussion. Barnes' instructional model consists of the following steps:

1. *Focusing stage*—Topic presented to full class. Teacher focuses upon the topic, encourages pupils to verbalize necessary preliminary knowledge, and if appropriate demonstrates assigned group work.

2. *Exploratory stage*—Pupils manipulate materials and discuss issues to which their attention has been directed.

3. *Reorganizing stage*—Teacher refocuses attention, tells groups how they will be reporting back, and establishes a time-frame.

4. *Public stage*—Groups present their findings to one another for further discussion.[6]

The instructional sequence suggested by Barnes ensures "an active participant in the making of meaning." The teacher's role as "transmitter of knowledge" changes to that of an "interpreter," who assists the learner in reshaping systematic and relevant knowledge from previous experience.[7]

---

[6] Douglas Barnes, *From Communication to Curriculum* (England: Penguin Books, 1975), p. 197.

[7] Barnes, p. 31.

A new school language policy will undoubtedly affect the uses of language as well as instructional approaches. To consciously manipulate language use in the classroom, an awareness of the conceptual and linguistic demands made of pupils and a knowledge of the pupils' linguistic resources are required.

Linguistic Demands in the Classroom: A Questionnaire for Teachers*

Program participant _____Grade/Subject _____

Part I. Please indicate the degree to which your students are involved in the following language activities. Place an "x" under the appropriate column for each type of activity.

Language Activities	Never	Once a semester	Once a month	Once a week	Daily
Speaking:					
• Making oral reports					
• Responding to teacher's questions					
• Participating in small-group discusion					
• Participating in panel discussions					
• Role-playing/dramatizations					
• Other:					
Writing:					
• Writing in a journal					
• Answering questions at end of chapter					
• Making outlines					
• Taking notes					
• Doing research/ term papers					
• Writing 5-paragraph essays					

* Developed in 1979 by Ramirez and Bayer for the Teacher Corps Project at Stanford University/San Jose Unified School District.

Language Activities	Never	Once a semester	Once a month	Once a week	Daily
• Writing letters • Writing poetry • Other:					
Reading: • Textbooks • Reference materials (atlas, encyclopedia) • Paperback books • Magazines • Maps, charts • Film • Filmstrips • Television • Other:					
Listening: • Class lectures • Guest speakers • Student presentations • Taped materials • Other:					

Part II. Please indicate the primary reasons for which your students are involved in the following language activities. Place an "x" under the appropriate column for each type of activity.

Language Activities	Present new materials	Motivate students	Review content	Evaluate learning	Improve mastery of English
Speaking • Making oral reports • Responding to teacher questions • Participating in small-group discussions • Role-play/dramatizations • Other:					

Language Activities	Present new materials	Motivate students	Review content	Evaluate learning	Improve mastery of English
Writing • Writing in a journal • Answering questions at end of chapter • Making outlines • Taking Notes • Doing research/term papers • Writing 5-paragraph essays • Writing letters • Writing poetry • Other:					
Reading • Textbooks • Reference materials (atlas, encyclopedia) • Paperback books • Newspapers • Magazines • Maps, charts • Film • Filmstrips • Television • Other:					
Listening • Class lectures • Guest speakers • Student presentations • Taped materials • Other:					

A Questionnaire for Pupils*

1. Write down the meaning of the following words:
    a. Living _____
    b. Animal _____
    c. Dissolve _____
    d. Refer _____
    e. Compare _____
    f. Distinguish _____
    g. Similar _____
    h. Concentrate _____
    i. Temperature _____

2. Which of the following techniques help you learn?

    Always   Often   Sometimes   Rarely   Never

    - Talking with the teacher
    - Talking in pairs
    - Talking in groups
    - Answering questions
    - Asking questions
    - Copying from board
      or books
    - Writing up experiments
    - Completing charts
    - Writing in your own words
    - Taking tests

3. How do you know if you have learned anything in science?

---

* From *Language Across the Curriculum: Guidelines for Schools* (London: Ward Lock Educational, 1977), p. 21.

Organizations That Can Help

Center for Applied Linguistics. Applies the findings of linguistic science to the solution of educational and social problems. (Contact the Center for Applied Linguistics, 3520 Prospect Street, N.W., Washington, D.C. 20007.)

National Clearinghouse for Bilingual Education. A federally supported organization established to provide information to teachers, project directors, administrators, and researchers on all aspects of bilingual education. (Contact NCBE, 1300 Wilson Boulevard, Suite B2-11, Rosslyn, Virginia 22209.)

Teachers of English to Speakers of Other Languages. A national organization that periodically publishes guidelines for teacher preparation programs, which may be useful in the selection process. (Contact TESOL, Georgetown University, 202 D.C. Transit Building, Washington, D.C. 20057.)

References

A Language for Life. London: Her Majesty's Stationery Office, 1975.

Barnes, Douglas. *From Communication to Curriculum.* England: Penguin Books, 1975.

Keen, John. *Teaching English, A Linguistic Approach.* London: Methuen and Co., Ltd., 1978.

Language Across the Curriculum: Guidelines for Schools. Southampton, England: National Association for the Teaching of English, 1977.

Marland, Michael, ed. *Language Across the Curriculum.* London: Heinemann Educational Books, 1977.

Richards, Jill. *Classroom Language: What Sort?* London: George Allen and Unwin, 1978.

Stubbs, Michael. *Language, Schools, and Classrooms.* London: Methuen and Co., Ltd., 1976.

Wood, Barbara Sundene. *Development of Functional Communication Competencies: Grades 7-12.* Urbana, Illinois: ERIC Clearinghouse on Reading and Communication Skills, 1967.

3.

Oral Communication

Don M. Boileau

The failure of students to learn and perform well in school frequently reflects weakness in basic communication skills—reading, writing, computation, listening, and speaking—more than it reflects their inability to master subject matter. These basic skills are the way students communicate mastery of content. If the basics are not mastered, inappropriate grades and inaccurate teacher impressions result. Although students spend 75 percent or more of their communication time speaking and listening, only 60 percent of high schools offer some classes in speech communication and less than 20 percent require such classes. As the satellite communication system increases our oral communication capability across the nation and around the world, the need for competency in the basic skills of speaking and listening becomes imperative.

Why Speaking and Listening are Part of the Basic Skills

Most communication time for the average person is spent in listening and speaking. An enlarged scope of functional communication provides the focus for contemporary speech communication courses that help the student produce messages by talking and receive messages by listening. Oral communication instruction, when properly developed, includes one-to-one, interpersonal communication; one-to-a-few in small groups; one-to-many in public speaking; and one-to-a-mass through the mass media.

Speech communication, like reading and writing, is meaning-centered. All three of these skills share a concern for information that the receiver understands, since the goal of oral and written communication is the transfer of meaning. The oral context provides a different set of circumstances from the written context for producing meaning. For example, the student

31

who complains to the vice principal about "this lousy school" creates a different set of meanings from one who writes the same words on the bathroom walls. Different meanings result from reading the words of a song in contrast to hearing them sung by the school choir. The oral context requires not only development of different skills, but also provides a wide range of challenges to the student in developing competence.

The unity of basic skills stems from the language and thinking processes that undergird them. Thus, it is important that oral communication instruction is systematically related to reading and writing instruction. For example, the organizational structure of a paragraph and the "one-point" speech share some of the same rhetorical concerns. Students benefit when they can develop structure in both writing and speaking and then apply these thought processes while reading what has been written by another person. This relationship of the basics is clarified by effective teachers. In a study of Michigan speech classes, 82 percent of the instructors were found to grade students on both oral and written performances—an excellent way to encourage the basic skills.

The skill of listening is as important for lectures as the skill of reading is for textbooks. Unless the student correctly processes the desired message, much instructional time is lost. Each time a teacher lectures, regardless of subject matter, the school can work to improve critical listening. What teachers rarely do is to check, except through a test later in the course, whether the student has absorbed the important ideas of the lecture. Teachers assume the secondary student knows how to listen, evaluate critically, and outline the material. Because listening is an often-neglected communication skill, teachers—just as they would check the spelling and punctuation on an essay—need to make sure students identify in their notes the same points the teacher has stressed in the lecture.

Like the nonreader who may have trouble reading material for a test or writing an essay based on readings, the reticent (speech-apprehensive) student may have trouble handling oral interactions in a group project in biology or government classes. Most schools have personnel, materials, and courses for the student with a reading problem. The student with a severe speech production problem (the largest of the eight groups of handicapping conditions in the school) can receive help from the speech and language therapist. But the quiet student with speech apprehension typically avoids the speech elective and thus misses the opportunity for needed help. As a result, the reticent student is often evaluated on the lack of a basic skill, rather than on mastery of content. In *Quiet Children and the Classroom Teacher,* McCroskey offers suggestions and strategies that range from using seating arrangements to oral reading to help the speech-reticent student.[1] Since estimates of such students reach 10 percent, schools should ascertain what is being done for them.

What are the Goals and Competencies for Speaking and Listening?

In 1978 Bassett and others produced a list of 19 basic competencies for speaking and listening.[2] These competencies, activities, and rationales can help supervisors work with teachers, curriculum committees, or departments. The goals serve as excellent statements to inform the school board and community about the basic skills component of the speech communication program. Teachers can use these 19 competencies to develop general educational objectives and specific course objectives. There are four main groups within which the 19 competencies fall.

Communication codes—skills that deal with minimal abilities in speaking and understanding spoken English and using nonverbal signs, such as gestures and facial expressions. The competencies include:

1. Listen effectively to spoken English.
2. Use words, pronunciation, and grammer appropriate for the situation.
3. Use nonverbal signs appropriate for the situation.
4. Use voice effectively.

Oral message evaluation—skills for making judgments about oral messages or their effect.

5. Identify main messages.
6. Distinguish facts from opinions.
7. Distinguish between informative and persuasive messages.
8. Recognize when another does not understand your message.

---

[1] James C. McCroskey, *Quiet Children and the Classroom Teacher* (Urbana, Ill.: ERIC/RCS Speech Communication Association, 1977).

[2] Ronald E. Bassett and others, "The Basics in Speaking and Listening for High School Graduates: What Should be Assessed?" *Communication Education* (November 1978): 322-327. The 19 skills of speaking and listening are contained in the pamphlet, "The SCA Guidelines for Minimal Competencies in Speaking and Listening for High School Graduates," available from the Speech Communication Association, 5105 Backlick Road, #E, Annandale, Virginia 22003.

Figure 1. Sample Competencies and Examples for Classroom Application

Competency	Occupational	Citizenship	Maintenance
9. Express ideas clearly and concisely.	Make a report to your job supervisor.	Describe a desired course of political action.	Explain appliance malfunction to a repair person.
	Explain job requirements to a new employee.	Describe an accident or crime to a policeman.	Explain an unfamiliar task to a child or other family member.
	State clearly relevant information about your work experience when applying for a job.	Explain citizens' rights to another.	Explain your values to your child or a friend.
10. Express and defend with evidence your point of view.	Express and defend your view in a union meeting.	Express and defend your view in a political discussion.	Express and defend your refusal to accept products or services you didn't order.
	Express and defend your suggestions for changes in job condition.	Express and defend your innocence in court.	Express and defend your faith or religion.
	Express and defend your reasons for job absence to your employer.	Express and defend your position in a city council meeting.	Express and defend your feelings in a family discussion.

Basic speech communication—skills that concern the process of selecting message elements and arranging them to produce spoken messages.

9. Express ideas clearly and concisely.
10. Express and defend with evidence your point of view.
11. Organize messages so that others can understand them.
12. Ask questions to obtain information.
13. Answer questions effectively.
14. Give concise and accurate directions.
15. Summarize messages.

Human relations—skills for building and maintaining personal relationships and for resolving conflict.

16. Describe another's viewpoint.
17. Describe differences in opinion.
18. Express feelings to others.
19. Perform social rituals.

Each skill has nine sets of suggested situations for assignment development by the classroom teacher, as shown in Figure 1. These examples were defined as ways to achieve three main purposes that reflect how adults use speaking and listening:

Occupational. To be a contributing member of society, an individual should be able to obtain a job, learn job requirements, and perform job tasks adequately.

Citizenship. The continuation of our form of government depends on the citizen's ability to understand, discuss, and evaluate laws, governmental policy, and the views of others, as well as to express his or her own opinions.

Maintenance. Maintaining one's self and family requires adults to form and preserve social relationships, manage personal finances, perform consumer tasks, gain and preserve health, avoid injury, and participate in daily life and child rearing.

The suggestions for classroom application that appear in Figure 1 reflect activities that can be used in speech classes and in other classes as well. The focus of oral communication competence as a preparation for adult life includes a concern for the career education movement, developing participating citizens in a democracy, and preparing students for family roles. Such an approach can help the school communicate to the public the "basics" emphasis that a speech communication requirement can meet.

How are Oral Communication Skills Now Taught?

The basic skills in secondary oral communication are taught in three formats: (1) specific speech courses, (2) subparts of a required communications or English course, or (3) indirect coverage by oral activities in classes. Specific classes in speaking and listening are generally titled "Speech," "Oral Communication," or "Speech Communication." Most secondary speech courses reflect both speaking and listening activities in interpersonal communication, small groups, public speaking, and mass media. The essential factor of a speech class is oral performance—reading out loud, speaking to classmates, and listening to other students. As in writing and math classes, the student practices the skill, but the audience is immediate and the language used is judged by whether it is "instantly intelligible." The message is now; it cannot be reread or rewritten.

Speech Courses

State surveys demonstrate that the basic high school speech course generally lasts only a semester and emphasizes public speaking. Since less than one-fifth of secondary students are required to take any speech courses, most students lack the systematic training in speaking and listening that can be communication skill-builders for other courses.

Oral communication skills are also stressed in courses such as drama, advanced speech, debate, radio and television (mass media), oral interpretation, film, discussion, and interpersonal communication. Many students receive partial instruction through extracurricular speech and drama activities: debate, drama, student congress, individual events, speakers' bureaus, and local/national speaking contests for prizes and scholarships. For many students, 20 nights of rehearsal or a weekend forensic tournament provides more critiqued performances than the basic course can offer. Although these activities reach only some of the students and focus on only part of the skills, any assessment of the school's basic skills instruction should consider both courses and extracurricular programs.

English Courses

The second approach includes devoting part of the teaching units in a required English course to speaking and listening activities. These formal or informal units generally last three, six, or nine weeks. Sometimes they are integrated into English activities in oral book reports or readers theatre presentations of literature. Some teachers integrate the rhetorical principles of writing and speaking and use the speech unit to stress and practice the differences. These English course units are different from semester-long speech courses taught by certified speech communicators. The short units do *not* provide adequate time-on-task and should be considered only as reinforcement, just as writing must be practiced in other than composition courses.

Indirect Approaches

In some schools, listening and speaking are taught by non-language arts teachers. The need to reinforce speaking and listening skills, like mathematics and writing skills, occurs not only in specific secondary level courses but in other subjects as well. For example, one of the ten basic skills in mathematics recommended by the National Council of Supervisors of Mathematics is "the reading and interpreting of tables, charts, and graphs," skills that are also important in social science classes. Speaking and listening also require more than just the performances in speech classes to provide the necessary exposure to a variety of situations, purposes, audiences, formats, and styles. As the school looks at its basic skills program in speaking, listening, mathematics, reading, and writing, the same principle applies: systematic instruction for focused theory, practice, and criticism must be matched by application of all basic skills in several content areas.

The use of speaking and listening skills in other subjects provides application of skills essential to any basic skills program. Unfortunately, many schools rely *only* on application because of finances, declining faculty, lack of knowledge about speech programs, or the shortage of speech teachers. This step meets application needs and improves content area development, but it does not fulfill the objective of teaching oral communication as an identifiable part of the curriculum.

Good teachers use oral performance as an exciting way to provide valuable instruction in their classes. Frequently the lab work in science is aided by good communication in the small groups assigned to a specific experiment. Role playing in the history class may draw upon drama, while orally reading a play in a readers theatre may bring literature alive. Oral reports and symposiums provide opportunities to speak in history class. The demonstration speech in sewing or electronics provides key ways to share the pride and process of the term project. If the school does not pursue in non-language arts classes these basic skills—whether they be writing or speaking, listening or reading—then student progress stagnates.

Examples of Secondary Schools with Oral Communication Programs

The following schools use a variety of approaches to teach oral communication aspects of the basic skills. These schools reflect "a required course mode," "optional courses within a speech requirement model," and "required units of an English requirement."

Fremont Union High School District, Sunnyvale, California. All students are required to take "Basic Oral Communication," which covers basic forms of public speaking (the speech to inform, to persuade), interpersonal discussion, the interview, business contacts, parliamentary procedure, and oral reading. Concerns for correct grammar, outlining, vocabulary, and research are integrated into the forms of communication that are covered. As a substitution, advanced students can take a full year of speech and debate classes. Other required English courses are two semesters of writing and two semesters of reading (literature). Advanced speech courses are part of the one and a half units of electives that complete the four-year requirement. This school is a model for basic skills since its unified basic skills approach requires every course receiving English credit for graduation to teach reading, writing, speaking, and listening skills.

Livonia Stevenson High School, Livonia, Michigan. In all four high schools in the district, ninth-grade students are required to take "Language Arts 9," a two-semester course in basic communication skills that devotes six weeks to developing oral communication skills. Tenth, eleventh, and twelfth-grade students must take five semesters of communication courses for the English requirement, two of which are in writing skills, two in literature, and one in oral communication. Students may choose among the following courses for the oral communication requirements: "Speech" (covering the basics in a survey of speaking and listening skills), "Public Speaking" (an advanced course for those with competency skills or those who have passed the first course), "Drama I," "Advanced Dramatics," "Radio and Television I," "Advanced Radio and TV," "Debate," "Forensics" (individual events), and "Communication and Discussion Skills" (an interpersonal approach focusing on the basic needs of students). Depending on the individual school's faculty and facilities, these options vary some among the high schools in the district.

Henry Sibley High School, Mendota Heights, Minnesota. Students are required to take four semesters of courses that include one semester of written composition, two semesters of literature, and one semester of speech arts. The sophomore "American Literature and Communication" course stresses both written and oral communication to provide a unified basic skills approach. Three options are possible in the speech arts semester: "Fundamentals of Speech" (reflecting the basic skills orientation of a variety of activities), "Argumentation and Persuasion" (challenging skilled students by focusing on debate as a critical thinking process that demands performance), and "Acting and Stagecraft I" (a basic drama performance class). Advanced students are able to substitute a semester course in debate, which involves competitive speaking. Advanced speaking and drama courses are available for "enrichment" credit.

Seminole High School, Seminole, Florida. In the ninth grade a required course called "Communication Techniques" covers both written and oral communication. In grades 10 through 12 the student takes four semesters of required courses of which one semester is written composition, one semester is "American Literature," and two semesters are "Advanced Communication Skills" (basically grammar and writing). For the rest of the requirements, students must take three more semesters of English courses. A speech course may be used as one or more of the electives, or the student can take three speech courses for this option. The three courses from which the student must choose for the initial semester of speech are "Interpersonal Communication," "Public Speaking I" (a survey course of the basic skills in speech), or "Debate Class." Both the public speaking and the debate class have advanced sections (Public Speaking II and III).

State Standards

Because each school should develop its own standards for speaking and listening, the local adaptation is a district-level decision. State requirements vary from little or no mention to very specific definitions.

For example, in Arizona, the ninth-grade speaking skills are "Discusses reading with others," "Gives oral and written reports," and "Follows oral and written directions in class." Specific assignments and topics reflect directions of the local school. In Michigan, the ninth-grade speaking/listening skills are grouped into five areas with objectives listed under each one. The 20 objectives Michigan uses, in contrast to Arizona's approach, reflect an enlarged scope of speaking and listening as well as reinforce many thinking and language objectives of the reading and writing program. Many of the objectives in Michigan were planned to dovetail with similar reading objectives. With either system, the teacher in the school must develop the specific assignments.

Perhaps you want the educational objective of a state program to be developed behaviorally for use in the classroom. The following two course objectives are models of speaking and listening objectives.

Speaking objective: *By the end of high school, the student will give a four-to-six-minute speech on a topic of his or her choice that has as its purpose to inform the audience. The speech will have at least (1) an introduction that has an attention getter and a statement of the thesis, (2) a development of the topic with two or more sections and at least three distinct types of supporting materials, and (3) a conclusion that summarizes and restates the thesis. The delivery will be characterized by appropriate eye contact with the audience, voice variation with appropriate volume, and directness of body movement. The language of the speech reflects clarity and vividness and an appropriate identification with the abilities and interests of the audience.*

Listening objective: *Given a recorded conversation between two people that discusses an emotion reaction to criticism of one person by another, the student can recall the main content of the situation, explain the emotion expressed in the para-language of one of the speakers, and identify the purpose of a speaker when the words and feelings are in conflict.*

The school can use these objectives to inform the public about how the school is meeting basic skills instruction. Details of an assignment are left to the teacher in teaching a general objective of a listening or speaking competency. For example, the model speaking objective above would fit the four dimensions of delivery, organization, content, and language, which are the basis of the Massachusetts Department of Education's "Speaking Assessment Ratings Guide." Such precision would probably not be applied in another subject-matter class, although the student who can reach the objective should do the science report or English book report with greater skill after such instruction.

An important part of both writing and speaking is the concern for "appropriateness" of speech in various parts of the country. For example, what might be too fast a rate in the South may be normal in the New England area. The word choice of students in the Southwest who might use Spanish terms common in that region would be different than in the upper Midwest states. The articulation of the "r" sound will vary. As part of listening, the effective teacher can include specific dialects of a geographical area to discover whether the student can follow the language that is spoken. Also, the teacher who uses the national media sources of listening exercises gives students exposure to the common language of the country. These differences only reinforce the importance of each district's having its own speaking and listening goals as part of the basic skills program.

Ways to Develop High School Programs

The first step for most schools is to determine the status of speaking and listening instruction and practice. The principal may want to establish a comprehensive basic skills assessment committee or limit the committee analysis to speaking and listening. In the comprehensive program, the committee may find it helpful to use an establish form, such as "Linguistic Demands in the Classroom" (see Ramirez's checklist on pp. 26-28 in Chapter 2).

Direct assessment of speaking can be done in several ways. The first criteria is passing an oral communication course that requires making a speech, such as the one outlined in the model objective. An integrated requirement like that of Fremont High School has a program dimension that can be checked.

Secondly, a quantifiable measurement is available using the two approaches developed by the Massachusetts Department of Education. The "Teacher Observational Approach" [3] requires that two teachers who had the same student in the same semester rate the student's general speaking performance in class. The "One-on-One" assessment by trained evaluators requires that the student speak on a given task (a description, an emergency, a sequence, or a persuasion task) and then be rated on a scale of 1 to 4 on the dimensions of delivery, organization, content, and language. Such scores are valuable in measuring the strength of the program and plotting progress over the years.

A third assessment, which is an easy indirect measure, is to poll the graduating seniors about how many stand-up-before-the-class speeches they made and how many group discussions they attended. What is listed in the curriculum guide and what students may actually have done may not be the same.

Some states have started programs for listening tests.[4] Michigan has tapes available that have been used to develop a statewide assessment

---

[3] Information on the administrative procedure, test development, score sheets, and testing data is available from the Massachusetts Department of Education (31 St. James Avenue, Boston, Massachusetts 02116).

[4] The National Assessment Program of the Education Commission of the States (1860 Lincoln Street, Denver, Colorado 80295) has done considerable background work on listening.

from a sample of schools. Students in Michigan listen to short excerpts from stories, radio announcements, and dialogues in order to answer questions related to eight listening objectives. Commercial tests are also available. In using listening tests, evaluators should be aware of the tendency to measure simpler skills of recalling information and identifying the main idea rather than measuring empathic listening skills. Some schools design their own tests to reflect local concerns and materials.

Recognizing the need for each district to develop its own objectives and to have a set of standards to begin evaluation, the Speech Communication Association and the American Speech-Hearing-Language Association jointly developed "Standards for Effective Oral Communication Programs." [6] These standards provide guidelines for a school to develop its own objectives by covering "Basic Assumptions," "Teaching and Learning," "Support," and "Assessment and Evaluation."

Oral communication facilitates instruction in all subjects. The student facing difficulties in speaking and listening is as handicapped as the student with reading and writing problems. Because secondary teachers use the lecture far more than do elementary teachers, practice in better listening should occur in all classrooms. Industry's recent emphasis on listening reinforces the need for this basic skill development. Activities that use oral communication not only provide variety for most classes, but they also give an experiential dimension that facilitates learning.

Teacher Preparation

For many schools, the key in developing an effective speech program is in obtaining and hiring a capable staff. The major concern in the first standard of support of the Speech Communication Association and the American Speech-Hearing-Language Association is that oral communication instruction be provided by individuals who are adequately trained in oral communication and/or communication disorders, and who have appropriate certification. Since the majority of secondary speech teachers are certified in both speech and English, hiring people with training in both fields provides the greatest flexibility. Frequently, a person who has taught English for many years may have the certification desired, although principals and supervisors ought to encourage some additional work and study in speech if the person has not worked in speech or kept up with the professional literature.

---

[5] The list of "Standards for Effective Oral Communication Programs" is available from the Speech Communication Association, 5105 Backlick Road, #E, Annandale, Virginia 22003.

Schools that are faced with declining enrollments and cannot hire new people should try to have one or two English teachers work toward a speech certificate. Most universities training speech teachers have night and summer programs oriented to teachers' needs. Each April the Speech Communication Association prepares a national list of workshops for teachers (61 such programs in 28 states were listed in 1981). Comprehensive speech programs typically use two speech teachers, one hired to coach debate and individual events and the other to direct dramatic productions. A third person in radio/television is an optional extension. The second pattern of combinations for certification exists within the social sciences. Since English and social studies are both areas with many classes to be taught, hiring for these positions should include one or more speech persons.

Inservice Development

The training of all teachers in communication competence is a major need. Schools might consider several options: (1) having local (or cross-district) speech and writing teachers hold small sessions on an inservice day so that non-language arts teachers can help students practice what is taught in writing and speaking classes; (2) having an outside speaker help develop oral assignments for specific groups of teachers so that content is integrated for subject matter areas (such as "Speech in Science Classes"); (3) holding a schoolwide inservice on general communication skills of teachers to reflect "Communication in the Classroom"; or (4) having specific communication-related courses taught in the district. School districts can contact the speech communication department of a local university or the state speech association to find people who are willing to help.

Extracurricular Activities

One important ingredient in the high school is the extracurricular program. It reaches the language development goals of active pupil-to-pupil dialogue related to subject matter. Debate, drama, and individual events function as extensions of the classroom. Adolescents learn and strengthen their knowledge of language by using language. Such activities allow considerable time for these opportunities. Many gifted students find challenges and ways to be recognized in such programs. Although extracurricular speech and drama activities do not reach all students the way a required course does, they do provide an important extension of practice for any school program and, as such, should be considered part of the development program in basic skills.

References

Allen, R. R., and Brown, Kenneth L., eds. *Developing Communication Competence in Children.* Skokie, Ill.: National Textbook Company, 1979.

Bassett, Ronald E., and others. "The Basics in Speaking and Listening for High School Graduates: What Should Be Assessed?" *Communication Education* (November 1978): 292-303.

Book, Cassandra L. "Teaching Functional Communication Skills in the Secondary Classroom." *Communication Education* (November 1978): 322-327.

Brown, Kenneth, and others. *Assessment of Basic Speaking and Listening Skills: State of the Art and Recommendations for Instructional Development.* CS 502 686. Boston: Massachusetts Department of Education, 1979.

"Communication Skills Chart: Speaking/Writing." Phoenix: Arizona State Department of Education, 1980.

"Communication Skills: Reading, Speaking/Listening, and Writing." Lansing: Michigan State Department of Education, 1977.

Del Polito, Carolyn M., and Lieb-Brilhart, Barbara. "Implications of Oral Communication as a Basic Skill." In *Education in the 80's: Speech Communication.* Edited by Gustav W. Friedrich. Washington, D.C.: National Education Association, 1981, pp. 123-130.

Larson, Carl, and others. *Assessing Functional Communication.* ED 153 275. Annandale, Va.: Speech Communication Association, 1978.

Lieb-Brilhart, Barbara. "Effective Oral Communication Programs: Myths and Tensions." In *Resources for Assessment in Communication.* Annandale, Va.: Speech Communication Association, 1980.

McCroskey, James C. *Quiet Children and the Classroom Teacher.* Urbana, Ill.: ERIC/RCS Speech Communication Association, 1977.

Wood, Barbara Sundene, ed. *Development of Functional Communication Competencies: Grades 7-12.* Urbana, Ill.: ERIC/RCS Speech Communication Association, 1977.

Reading

Judith Thelen

What is reading in the content area?

Reading in the content area means changing reading assignments so that the content teacher can teach the subject in such a way that the student can read about it with little or no difficulty. Many students are failing because they can't comprehend assigned reading from textbooks.

Does reading in the content area mean that every teacher is a teacher of reading?

No, not at all. "Every Teacher, A Teacher of Reading" was developed by reading specialists as a defense. Teachers of subjects other than reading complain that kids can't learn the subject matter because they can't read. The reading teacher, often feeling responsible for those reported reading levels, shifts the responsibility back to the content teachers with that phrase. The battle goes on—each side blaming the other.

Isn't that a legitimate concern?

Concern, yes. But both positions are a result of the dominant role that the textbook plays in instruction. Textbooks are not teachers! They should be used by teachers, not in place of them. That is what reading in the content area is all about—helping teachers use their textbooks.

Are you recommending that teachers get rid of their textbooks?

Absolutely not. The textbook is an excellent tool that teachers can use to reinforce or expand on what *they have taught*.

Do you recommend that teachers rewrite their textbooks at a lower level of difficulty?

No, teachers don't have time to do that. Besides, there is some evidence that suggests there may be no difference in achievement between classrooms using multilevel texts and those using one-level texts.[1]

What is the answer? Do you see this back-to-basics movement as a solution?

That depends. To some people, "basics" means that students should be taught skills to help them decode their language. These people feel that if students can pronounce the words, they will be able to read. The decoding sequence is to learn the sound of letters, to figure out syllables, and eventually to sound out words. Once the students can sound out the words, they will be able to read the textbook.

What's wrong with that?

It's not that easy. Knowing how to pronounce a word does not guarantee that one will know the meaning of the word. Many students can pronounce words but have no idea of what they mean. There is nothing more basic to reading than understanding or comprehending.

What is reading, then?

Reading is making sense out of what one reads.[2] When you have understood the author's message, we can say that you have read the message.

Isn't it essential that content teachers become reading teachers?

I don't think so. We are not suggesting the retrenchment of content teachers into reading teachers. A content teacher's job is to help students understand the concepts and principles of the subject taught. If the teacher uses a textbook to help teach those concepts and principles, then that teacher must have at hand ideas to assist the student in comprehending what is assigned.

---

[1] D. Daugs, "Influence of Multilevel Science Materials on Achievement of Sixth Grade Students," *Journal of Research in Science Teaching* 19 (1973): 147-152.

[2] F. Smith, *Understanding Reading* (New York: Holt, Rinehart and Winston, 1970).

What you're saying is that content area reading will help teachers help students comprehend. How?

To answer that, we have to talk about reading comprehension. Reading comprehension is a process. Reading comprehension means understanding printed language. It means using *prior experiences* to make sense out of that printed language.

You mean that to understand what one reads, one must know the language in which the material is written?

That goes without question; that is essential for understanding. By the time most students enter school, they are very adept at listening to and speaking their own language. Reading in the content area deals with helping students make sense out of *their printed* language.

How can we be sure that the student has the ability to deal with the language of the textbook?

A great deal of scholarly research has been done on a quick and efficient test that measures that ability. That test is called a cloze procedure, which is discussed in detail at the end of this chapter.

Consider this—when asked to complete this sentence: "I went swimming in the _____," most youngsters will respond with pool, ocean, water, creek, morning, lake, nude, or any other noun that makes sense. They may not be able to tell you that the word they replaced was a noun. They will put in a word that makes sense. Why? Because they have been users of their language for a long time. They are able to generate their own rules and respond correctly to questions on material that makes absolutely no sense to them at all. For example, second-graders were given the first stanza of Lewis Carroll's *Jabberwocky*:

> Twas brillig and
>   the slithy toves,
> Did gyre and gimble
>   in the wabe
> All mimsy were the
>   borogoves
> And the mome raths
>   out grabe.

They were asked: (1) What were the toves doing? and (2) Where were they doing it? Most of the youngsters responded, "The toves were gyring and gimbling in the wabe." Notice, even when they didn't understand the meaning of the words, they changed the tense of those words to match the tense expected by the question, "What were they doing?" "They were gyring and gimbling!" They do that because they are successful users of their language. They have learned to respond to their language. We are the ones who are fooled by those students who respond correctly to our literal level questions without even understanding the answers they give!

Can you relate an example from your secondary school experience?

I was working with some physical science teachers. One of the teachers told me that his students could read the textbook and answer his questions, but when they were asked to explain their answers they couldn't. I asked the students to read something from their text. They read, to themselves, this sentence: "In the melting process, ions of the melt collide with ions in the crystals and give those ions enough energy so that they escape from their potential wells; those ions enter the melt."[3] Then I asked them two questions. (1) What happened in the melting process? (2) What did the collision of the ions in the melting process do to the ions in the crystal? The students wrote, "The ions in the melt collided with the ions in the crystal" and, "The ions in the crystal were given enough energy to enable them to escape from their potential wells." But when I asked them to tell me what that meant, they couldn't. Although they used the language and changed tenses (without even knowing the rules for doing so), they didn't comprehend. The thought that was expressed in that language didn't make any sense to those students. They had no meaning for or prior experience with the words used by the author.

Let's go back to this notion of prior experience with the words used by the author. Some teachers introduce the new vocabulary before they give homework in the text. Is that what you mean by prior experience with the words used by the author?

Partially; and that is a good practice. However, I mean more than that. In that physical science lesson, I could have defined "ion" and "melt"; but I wonder if that would have given the readers enough information to comprehend the total lesson. So it isn't *just* vocabulary introduction. Prior knowledge or prior experience is what the learner already knows about the subject before you start to teach it.

---

[3] *An Approach to Physical Science: Physical Science for Nonscience Students* (New York: John Wiley and Sons, Inc., 1969), p. 410.

If the learner already knows, then why teach it?

I don't mean the concept, per se. I mean background experience that is relevant to the new material to be learned. I remember something a prominent science educator said about that: "There is a growing body of evidence to indicate that some reasonable degree of learning for most any concept can take place if proper instructional sequences are provided and examples and activities are used that will relate to the prior experience of the learner." [4]

You are saying prior experience is a concern of all teachers.

Yes. Not too long ago, math education specialists demonstrated in their research that it wasn't the ability to read the math problems that was causing difficulty for their students.[5] It was not knowing which operations to perform. That deals with prior knowledge! If a science teacher assigned a chapter on potential energy, students without any knowledge of energy would have difficulty relating to the new material. It probably would not make much sense to them. The same thing might be true if a math teacher wanted to teach the concept of absolute value. Students with no prior knowledge of a number line would have difficulty understanding absolute value. Learning should be meaningful. Relating what is read to what is known helps to make sense out of the printed text and helps to make it meaningful.

If new material doesn't make sense, students just memorize it?

Right. Other unpleasant things may occur, too. If what is read doesn't make sense, students become bored. Bored students may gradually withdraw from the learning situation by refusing to do their assignments, missing classes, and becoming discipline problems. They become everyone's concern.

How can content area reading help teachers help students make sense out of what they are expected to read?

One way of achieving meaningful reading is to request that teachers

[4] J. D. Novak, "Understanding the Learning Process and Effectiveness of Teaching Methods in the Classroom, Laboratory and Field," *Science Education* 60 (1976): 493-521.

[5] J. D. Knifong, and B. Holton, "An Analysis of Children's Writing Solutions to Word Problems," *Journal of Research in Mathematics* 106 (1976): 111.

change the way they assign materials. Most content teachers follow a model suggested by Margaret Early.[6]

ASSIGNMENT: OLD STYLE

Students are told to read the chapter for the next class. Some will; some won't; some can't. At the next class meeting, quite a bit of time is spent discussing the assignment with those who "claim" to have read it. Much of that time is spent clearing up misconceptions for those who did not understand and admonishing those who didn't (or couldn't) read it!

In this model isn't the textbook the primary source of information and the teacher the interpreter?

Surely. There are very few teachers who would abdicate their primary responsibility to teach the concepts of their respective disciplines. Yet, in this very popular model, the textbook has replaced the teacher.

You believe that teachers should change the way they assign materials. Will this new way of assigning materials take more time?

Not really. What we are asking teachers to do is to discuss what students read before they read it. In other words, prepare students by drawing on prior experiences they may have had with specific material.

---

[6] Developed by Margaret Early, presented at the Maryland IRA State Meeting in Baltimore, March 1980.

ASSIGNMENT: NEW STYLE

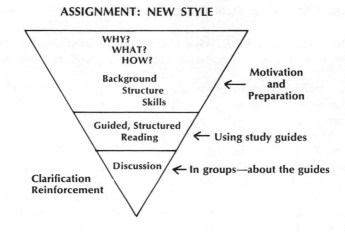

Are you suggesting that teachers not only have to teach the new concepts but also have to provide the relevant information that students should have gotten in elementary school?

That's not what I mean. I mean, for example, if a science teacher is going to teach *potential energy,* it would be worthwhile to find out what the students already know about *energy.* If students don't understand *energy,* it will be necessary to explain that concept before moving on to *potential energy.*

In another example, one teacher wanted to teach *King Lear* and *Hamlet* but wasn't sure what her students knew about Shakespearean tragedy. So, she talked about literature in general and drama in particular. As the discussion progressed, she put a diagram on the bulletin board to help provide a framework for *Hamlet.*

What if students didn't know anything about Shakespearean drama? Then what would happen?

Students watch television, don't they? Even if they don't know the term *drama,* they certainly have experienced it. Before teaching *Romeo and Juliet,* many English teachers show the film *West Side Story.* Then, before assigning the classic, they compare the characters from the two. In one case, the teacher told the students that Tony and Maria could be thought of as Romeo and Juliet in the new material to be learned. What that teacher was doing was relating the familiar to what was unfamiliar. English teachers using this model attempt to clear up misconceptions before the students read. That makes more time.

That's classroom time. What about pre-classoom time? It looks like this new way of assigning materials takes more pre-class planning.

Initially, it will. However, the first step should not take much more time than the old model. At first glance, the old model looks as if there were little or no teacher preparation. It appears that all a teacher has to do is assign the next chapter and answer the students' questions the next day. That is a dangerous assumption. In the old model, teachers must prepare for discussions following the reading. Even if it is nothing more than one chapter ahead of the students!

In this new model, the teacher decides before class what prior experiences students need to have before they can relate to the new material. How teachers aid the student in organizing the new material will depend on the difficulty of the concepts and the ability of the students.

Are there other strategies you can suggest to assist teachers in helping students organize their prior experiences?

There are many strategies that teachers can use before they assign material to be read. Some of these can be found in the bibliography. Some are recommended by Stallings in Chapter 1.

Do you believe that by providing some kind of structure before students read we can actually help those who are considered poor comprehenders?

Very definitely. In fact, there is quite a bit of research to support the importance of structuring prior experiences before reading assignments are made. Most of that research is cited in the recommended readings on page 58.

The Early Model suggests there are steps other than the preparation stage.

That's correct. Showing students how new concepts relate to other concepts in their prior experience is an important step in facilitating learning from assigned reading, but it may not be enough. Many students need guidance to comprehend the material. The guidance procedure helps students through the concept-forming processes.

How is that accomplished?

One way is through the use of study guides. It's not enough to tell students what to look for when assigning reading from a textbook. If we don't provide some guidance for those students with low verbal ability, they may memorize a few key terms or sentences without trying to understand what they mean. The recommended readings include several texts that provide study guides.

Isn't that spoonfeeding?

No, if by spoonfeeding you mean a process when parents still feed their children even though the children know how to feed themselves. In this case, we cannot assume that students know how to process the information in the text. Therefore, we must provide some kind of guidance.

How much guidance do we provide?

The kind and amount of guidance provided depends upon the learning task and the abilities of the students. Guidance ranges from simple to complex, depending on the students' ability, the level of difficulty of the text, and the level of comprehension the student is expected to attain. If we are only concerned with a literal comprehension of the material, then very little guidance is needed. Do you remember our "gyring" and "gimbling" students?

When are the guides given?

Guides may be required before the student reads, as the student reads, or after the student reads. They may not be required at all, in some cases. A study guide does not have to be designed for every assigned reading. Study guides should be used only when assigned reading presents potential difficulties for students.

Who writes these guides? Doesn't writing take time?

Written study guides are developed by the content teacher, often with the aid of a reading teacher. The content teachers know the content, and the reading educator knows the process. Of course, the content teacher can be trained in that process—and that is an essential part of content area reading. Writing study guides does take time. That part of the new model will take more pre-classroom time on the part of teachers.

Teachers already are complaining that there's not enough time in the day to accomplish what needs to be done.

Some school systems have given teachers time in the summer to construct materials—just before school opens. Other programs have obtained substitute-release time during the school year. That's all part of implementing a content reading program.

I am enthusiastic, but I need to know more before I can support it.

Such programs cannot be established overnight. You must take one step at a time. Programs cannot be mandated. I work with a teacher in Alaska who has been recognized by the International Reading Association for her outstanding content area reading program. She told me it took her three years to see the results of her efforts.

How did she begin?

She attributes much of the success of the program to her principal and vice-principal. At the time she went to them with her ideas, she was teaching six periods of reading. They reduced the number of her reading classes so that she was free for certain periods during the day to aid content teachers in developing preparation techniques and study guides.

Didn't some teachers complain because she didn't have a full teaching load?

I'm sure they did. But content area reading is a service. Once teachers saw results, they were happy. Don't get me wrong. Although content area reading is alive and well in her school, there are still a few teachers who are not sold on it. She also increased her credibility when she requested one class of social studies so that she could practice what she preached.

How should I begin?

Herber has recommended the following sequence for a successful program.[7]

1. Educate administrators and supervisors in how to teach reading

---

[7] H. L. Herber, "Reading Programs Grades 7-12," *Projections for Reading Preschool Through Adulthood,* HEW Publication No. OE 77-00110, 47-56 (1979).

in the content area so that their interaction with participating teachers will be informed and supportive.

2. Work carefully with an initial group of strong teachers who become resource teachers or "teacher trainers."

Did they do that in the Alaska program?

Very definitely. Some strong teachers in social studies and science eventually became "teacher trainers."

The next steps were also incorporated into the Alaska model:

3. Identify eager volunteers for inservice workshops with teacher trainers during released time (arranged by the supportive administrative staff).

4. Provide for follow-up sessions so that participants can react to their experiences, secure feedback, and study variations and modifications developed by their colleagues and others who are involved in the same program.

That's just one way of implementing a successful program. There are others from which to choose.

How does a content area reading program relate to basic skills?

Basic skills have been defined as "reading, mathematics, and effective communication, both oral and written." The back-to-basics movement was motivated by a number of things: low reading scores, poor writing skills, and mathematical incompetence. In other words, the public was telling us that students were not learning. Parents and others remembered their instruction in the basics and suggested that we return to them. To some, back-to-basics meant cutting out the frills and reducing the curriculum to the bare minimum: reading, writing, and arithmetic. They thought that if students could learn to read, they could learn any subject.

That makes sense, doesn't it?

Yes, but by learning to read, many people meant learning to decode words. Learn to pronounce words and you can read, they assumed. Pronouncing words is not reading; students can pronounce *gyre* and *gimble,* but pronunciation does not demonstrate comprehension.

A common characteristic of poor high school readers is that they read as if they do not expect what they read to make sense—as if getting every individual word right is the key to reading.[8] Reading is making sense out of printed material. Students who are not learning cannot make sense out of their assigned reading. The solution is not to go back to the basics, but to move forward. A program in content area reading is an attempt to do this.

The Cloze Test

Description and Construction

A cloze test is constructed by mutilating or deleting words from a selected passage that one intends to use for instruction. Mutilation is accomplished by randomly deleting every fifth word and replacing those words with 50 blanks of equal length (about one and a half inches). The test should start and end with a complete sentence.

Administration and Scoring

Cloze tests are distributed to students who are given oral instructions to read the mutilated passage and fill in all blanks, one word per blank, by determining the missing words from the context of the remaining words. A time limit should not be imposed on the test.

Perhaps the greatest feature of this test is the facility with which it is scored. Only when the exact word that was deleted is supplied is credit given. Research by Taylor [9] and Bormuth [10] indicates that when cloze tests are used as measures of individual differences in reading ability, scores obtained by counting exact replacements—not synonyms—more often yield value scores. Rankin and Culhane [11] note that counting synonyms makes scoring cumbersome and could lead to arbitrary decisions regarding the worth of the synonym as a replacement. Words spelled incorrectly should not invalidate a correct response.

A score between 41 percent and 60 percent usually means that the material is at the student's instructional reading level; that is, materials at this level are suitable if the student has guidance from a teacher.

---

[8] F. Smith, *Reading Without Nonsense* (New York: Teachers College Press, 1979), p. 34.

[9] W. S. Taylor, "Cloze Procedures: A New Tool for Measuring Readability," *Journalism Quarterly* 30 (1953): 415-431.

[10] J. R. Bormuth, "Comparable Cloze and Multiple Choice Comprehension Test Scores," *Journal of Reading* 10 (1967): 291-299.

[11] E. Rankin and J. Culhane, "Comparable Cloze and Multiple Choice Comprehension Test Scores," *Journal of Reading* 13 (1969): 193-198.

Papers with scores that fall below 40 percent should be carefully re-examined by the teacher. The cloze test is merely a screening device to separate levels of learners. Scores above 40 percent indicate that students have supplied appropriate replacements for deleted words and will probably not have much difficulty reading the book at the literal level. Scores below 40 percent do not necessarily mean that the student will have difficulty reading the material. On the contrary, the examiner may discover that the student has chosen better or more appropriate synonyms than the author of the passage. It is appropriate, at this time, to read for synonyms. If the student has not written appropriate or relevant synonyms, the teacher can expect that the student will have difficulty reading the textbook. A cloze score above 60 percent usually indicates that the material is easy enough for the student to read without assistance.

Sample Cloze Test

Cloze description and construction. A cloze test is constructed by mutilating or deleting words from a selected text passage that one intends to use for instruction. Mutilation _____ accomplished by randomingly deleting _____ fifth word and replacing _____ words with 50 blanks _____ equal length (about 1½ _____). The test should start _____ end with a complete _____.

Cloze administration and scoring. Cloze tests _____ distributed to students who _____ oral instructions to read _____ mutilated passage and fill _____ all blanks, one word _____ blank, by determining the _____ words from the context _____ the remaining words. A _____ limit should not be _____ on the test.

Perhaps _____ greatest feature of this _____ is the facility with _____ it is scored. Only _____ the exact word that _____ deleted is supplied is _____ given. Research by Taylor _____ Bormuth indicates that when _____ tests are used as _____ of individual differences in reading _____, scores obtained by counting _____ replacements—not synonyms—often _____ valid scores. Rankin and _____ note that counting synonyms _____ scoring cumbersome and could _____ to arbitrary decisions regarding _____ worth of the synonym _____ a replacement. Words spelled _____ should not invalidate a _____ response.

Papers with _____ that fall below 40 _____ should be carefully re-examined _____ the teacher. The cloze test is merely a screening device to separate levels of learners.

Recommended Reading

Earle, R. *Teaching Reading and Mathematics.* Newark, Del.: International Reading Association, 1976.

Estes, T., and Vaughn, J. *Reading and Learning in the Content Classroom.* Boston: Allyn and Bacon, 1979.

Herber, H. *Teaching Reading in the Content Areas.* 2nd ed. New Jersey: Prentice-Hall, 1978.

Lunstrum, J., and Taylor, B. *Teaching Reading in the Social Studies.* Newark, Del.: International Reading Association, 1978.

Thelen, J. *Improving Reading in Science.* Newark, Del.: International Reading Association, 1976.

Tierney, R.; Readance, J.; and Dishner, E. *Reading Strategies and Practices: Guide for Improving Instruction.* Boston: Allyn and Bacon, 1980.

Vacca, R. *Content Area Reading.* Boston: Little, Brown, 1981.

5.

Writing

Arthur N. Applebee

The Writing Problem and Its Sources

The National Assessment of Educational Progress (NAEP) recently characterized 10 to 25 percent of 17-year-olds as having "massive problems with written language." [1] Three quarters of the students studied could write a competent narrative, but only half were successful at an explanatory writing task, and only 15 percent at a persuasive writing task. The achievement gap between urban and black students and the rest of the nation narrowed from 1969 to 1979, but American secondary school students' overall achievement level remained essentially constant.

Some commentators put the blame for these appalling statistics on such external factors as television and social ills. Much of the problem, however, stems from our failure to give writing a recognized place in the curriculum. Students simply are not asked to write often enough. When they do write, they receive little helpful instruction. In the National Assessment, for example, less than half of the 17-year-olds had written as many as four papers in the six weeks prior to the assessment. Only 7 percent routinely received instruction that would help them with the writing process.

These reports from students are reinforced by the results from the National Study of Writing in the Secondary Schools,[2] which found that only about 3 percent of secondary school students' class time or homework

---

[1] NAEP has published a series of national reports on writing achievement at various age levels. Items from the assessment can be adapted for school use (see the resource section of this chapter for NAEP's address).

[2] Arthur Applebee, *Writing in the Secondary School: English and the Content Areas* (Urbana, Ill.: National Council of Teachers of English, 1981).

assignments (in all subjects) involve writing. Instead, multiple-choice exercises, short-answer questions, and a variety of worksheet formats abound. These tasks all involve some variety of written language, but the teacher assumes the problems of organization and synthesis, leaving students to "fill in" missing information that can be graded as "right" or "wrong."

When students are asked to write, the teacher typically assigns a topic, indicates an appropriate length, and selects a due date; the rest students do themselves. English teachers are more likely to teach specific writing skills than are other teachers, but even in English most instruction occurs after the fact. Teachers comment extensively on completed work rather than helping students while they are planning or drafting. Second drafts, in which students can respond to teachers' suggestions, are rarely required in any subject.

Examining Your School's Writing Program

When assessing the value of your school's writing program, you can watch for the following "danger signals."

Danger Signal 1: Low or falling scores on writing tests

Schools typically gather an enormous amount of measurement data on student achievement. If your school has an effective writing program, test scores should reflect its effectiveness. Remember, many standardized tests of writing actually measure more limited skills, such as editing ability. The most appropriate scores to consider are those based on actual student writing samples. These may come from regular schoolwide writing assessments or from state or local writing competency tests.[3]

If you judge your writing program on the basis of student performance on mandated competency exams, remember that the level of achievement needed to pass such exams is usually very low; in an effective writing program, the only students who should have any difficulty passing are those with perceptual handicaps or other learning disabilities, or those whose native language is not English.

If you don't have a direct measure of writing achievement available, you can get some information from tests of related skills—usage, vocabulary, and editing skills—and from standardized achievement tests, college entrance examinations, or competency tests that do not require writing samples. Such scores tend to rise or fall as writing achievement improves

---

[3] Miles Myers, *A Procedure for Writing Assessment and Holistic Scoring* (Urbana, Ill.: National Council of Teachers of English, 1980).

or deteriorates. The danger in relying only on such measures, however, is that it can lead to inappropriate changes in the curriculum. Focusing on usage exercises, for example, will raise test scores on usage tests but it won't improve writing achievement.

Danger Signal 2: Easily-graded objective tests in wide use for major school examinations

Midterm and final examinations make an important statement about the knowledge the school values. In many schools, the ease and efficiency of multiple-choice and short-answer formats lead to their adoption for major examinations. Although easy to grade, these tests tell students indirectly that the ability to write about what they have learned isn't important. This is unfortunate because writing about subject matter is one of the better ways to assess students' ability to apply new concepts and integrate new information in any subject. If English classes are the only place where students are required to write, they will have little motivation to improve their writing abilities. Examinations requiring writing can be a strong motivation for mastering writing skills.

Danger Signal 3: Omission of writing from schoolwide assessments

If the school routinely assesses student achievement through standardized tests or competency examinations, writing skills should be among the areas assessed. Such assessment should be based on samples of student writing, not on indirect, objective indices of writing ability. Well-designed assessments of writing serve several functions: they emphasize the importance of writing; they enable you to monitor long-term changes in the effectiveness of your program; and they provide diagnostic information about student strengths and weaknesses. Each student's cumulative record should include results of writing assessments along with other achievement measures.

Danger Signal 4: Support systems do not provide services to students with writing problems

Whether your school uses special education teachers, tutoring, remedial classes, or reduced class size for the lowest achievers, it should give attention to students who need help with their writing. Although reading programs and reading teachers sometimes provide help with writing, most reading teachers have neither the training to work with writing problems, nor the appropriate instructional approaches or materials for teaching writing. And they lack the time in already crowded schedules to take on new responsibilities.

**Danger Signal 5: Complaints by students or teachers about low
levels of writing achievement**

If students or teachers are concerned about "the writing problem," your school is in a position to implement a more effective program regardless of achievement levels.

Steps to Improve Writing Instruction

Step 1: Mobilize interest in improving writing instruction

An effective writing program requires the involvement of the entire school; it cannot be accomplished simply by revising the English curriculum. If any of the danger signals are present in your school, you might begin by convening a small group of interested teachers to study the extent of the problem. Although the English department will have the most expertise in teaching writing, it is essential to involve leaders from other departments—they know the kinds of writing skills that are important in their own subject areas, and they can suggest changes within their own departments.

A simple assessment of the amount of writing students do can be a powerful device for mobilizing interest in more effective programs. A small number of cooperative students can be asked to save their written work for one or two weeks. Written work should include class notes, rough work that is later recopied, exercises, worksheets, and more extensive writing. Several things usually emerge in such a study: (1) the total number of words that students write in a week will be surprisingly low, perhaps only a few hundred words; (2) most of the collected writing will involve filling in information rather than constructing a coherent piece of prose; (3) students who write well are most likely to be given writing assignments; those who need the most help will get the least practice; (4) the amount of student writing will vary considerably depending upon the particular combination of teachers each student has; (5) there will be little evidence of progression in writing tasks from grade-to-grade or consistency from teacher-to-teacher even within the same grade and subject. Any one of these findings can serve as a catalyst for discussion and change.

Step 2: Encourage a schoolwide emphasis on writing

Writing should be part of a student's work in all areas of the curriculum. This will not happen if teachers view "writing across the curriculum" only as a way to improve writing ability (or perhaps to help the English department). Teachers in other content areas must come to view writing as important to their own goals rather than as additional work displacing part of their "real" curriculum.

Writing is a powerful tool for organizing and synthesizing new information. When teachers prepare short-answer or fill-in-the-blank exercises, they are really doing much of the writing task for the student, reminding students how one bit of information relates to another. If students are forced to reconstruct these relationships for themselves—to realize that A caused B, but that C almost upset the whole process—they develop a much firmer grasp of both the new information and the underlying concepts. Language contains many devices that help students discover new meaning. These devices take many shapes: they include the *buts,* the *ands,* and the *althoughs* that relate one set of information to another; they include the basic grammatical relationships of subjects, objects, and predicates; and they include structural devices underlying larger stretches of writing—such as time sequence in narrative, or generalization and supporting detail in exposition. Students should be given the opportunity to practice using these devices in all areas of their learning.

Each subject area has its own vocabulary and modes of argument. Writing a scientific report is a different task from writing an historical essay, and both are different from writing a critical analysis of a novel or short story. Students need to learn more than the "facts" involved in a subject; they also need to master the specialized vocabulary and modes of expression that are appropriate to each field.

The important point is that writing has many uses outside the English curriculum. Students take notes on their reading in history, write lab reports in chemistry, provide "how-to-do-it" instructions in shop or auto mechanics, compile recipes in domestic science, explain theorems or heuristics in mathematics classes, write essays or stories in their foreign language classes, and so on. Teachers in all classes need to be reminded that they are not taking time from their "real" work to teach writing; they are enriching their teaching by using writing for their own purposes.

Step 3: Resist efforts to solve the writing problem with a remedial writing class

It is easy to respond to "writing problems" with a "problem class."

Effective writing instruction, however, requires a carefully planned, developmental program in which students learn to write in a variety of genres for diversified audiences. Such a writing program should be fully integrated into every student's English curriculum, not isolated as a special class for students with problems.

Effective writing involves many different skills, from the mechanics of spelling, punctuation, and sentence structure to the rhetorical and organizational skills necessary to tell an engaging story or to build an effective argument. Mechanical errors are highly visible and easily seized upon by critics of a school. But an effective program must keep writing skills in perspective, as means to other ends. Students must learn to write for real purposes and to convey messages or construct arguments for readers who will respond to what has been said as well as to how it has been said. Because writing is a complex task, many of the errors in student work are actually reflections of learning-in-progress; students who make no "mistakes" may be using old skills rather than learning new ones.

In addition to a well-planned, sequential program, students need a place to go when they are having problems with a writing assignment. Some of the most effective "safety nets" are built around a "Writing Center" that is available to all students, not just to those who are "failing." A Writing Center can provide appropriate remedial help for students who need it, but it can also guide capable students who are tackling more complex writing tasks. Although a Writing Center is likely to be staffed with English teachers who have had special training in the teaching of writing, it can be a resource for work in all subjects. If students of all levels of writing ability are encouraged to come for help when they need it, some of the stigma of being in a "remedial class" is removed from those students who may need the most help.

By focusing your attention on the overall writing program, rather than only on eradicating errors or providing remedial instruction, you can help your instructional staff maintain a similar balance and perspective.

Step 4: Reward good writing

Good writing requires hard work and personal commitment. Teachers share interesting papers with individual classes in a number of ways ranging from bulletin boards and ditto machines to reading passages aloud or providing class time to exchange papers. It is important that these in-class activities are reflected throughout the school. School newspapers, magazines, and year books are forums for student writing and should be actively supported by the administration, not just tolerated or ignored.

They not only provide young writers with a real audience, but can improve the school's image in the community.

School publications are not the only way to increase the prestige of young writers, however. Annual writers' conferences can be organized, and community assistance from the parents association can be enlisted. Although such conferences often emphasize creative writing, they can include other categories of competition such as science reporting, history essays, and so on. If the categories are broad enough, and if the conference emphasizes "good writing" rather than "the best writer," a writers' conference can recognize and encourage many students instead of just a handful of "the best."

Schools can also participate in state, regional, and national contests that emphasize writing. As deadlines for nominations approach, judges of an in-school competition can select the nominees for the larger contest. Schools should publicize "winners" at each step of the process; it is not necessary to have a national "winner" to reward good writing.

Similarly, you can show students that writing has a valued place in the adult world. In many parts of the country, active "Poets-in-the-Schools" programs allow successful poets to work with students. The same format can be used to introduce students to the techniques of writers in other fields such as journalism, publishing, advertising, and the media. Time spent with professionals shows students that writing does matter.

Step 5: Ensure a place for writing when your school adopts new instructional technologies

Schools tend to adopt new technologies first in the "technical" subjects, such as science and mathematics, where teachers are likely to be comfortable with machines. The rapid development of microcomputer technology in the last decade, for example, has affected more mathematics and business education classes than English and humanities courses. Yet with administrative support and encouragement, investments in such equipment can have much broader benefits.

At the simplest level, microcomputers can help students improve particular mechanical skills through a variety of games and exercises. Such help can be completely individualized and yet, because it is controlled by a machine, free the teacher's energies for more complex problems.

At another level, many of the machines available for school use have word processing and text editing options that are particularly helpful to students learning about the writing process. Humanities departments as well as the sciences should explore these resources with their students.

The novelty of working on the computer can motivate the weaker student, while some of the available software can also help these students recognize simple errors and expedite revisions. For academically oriented students, the ability to work with these machines may soon be as much of a "survival skill" as personal typewriting.

Step 6: Capitalize on community concern about writing

If you restructure your writing program, you will probably do it in a context of community concern. Often the community expresses concern through editorials or letters from parents who deplore falling standards and cite examples of students' spelling and mechanical errors. Their concern is legitimate and provides the opportunity for building community involvement in your program. School boards, parents' associations, school newspapers, and sometimes even reports or columns in local newspapers all provide outlets for discussing issues in the teaching of writing. In particular, when the community is interested in students' writing ability, it is possible to develop a richer notion of "good writing" and the components of a "good" program. Parents' interest in their children's writing is a potent source of motivation. If they understand the goals of the school program, they can reinforce those goals throughout a child's school career.[4]

Step 7: Support inservice work on the teaching of writing

Even when teachers are interested in improving instruction, they may simply not know how to go about it. In this situation, you may have to insist that your staff draw on outside help in reformulating the writing program; otherwise, there is a danger that solutions will simply be larger doses of old and familiar approaches.

Expertise can be provided in a variety of ways. Sometimes a teacher will be interested enough to take formal courses at a local college or university. Released time or tuition payments to support such work may be well worth the investment if the teacher returns to take a leadership role in rebuilding your school's writing program. You may want to bring in outside consultants to work with the English department or other interested teachers, as well as to help you interpret new programs to the school board and other community groups. In general, you can benefit more from a relatively long-term commitment from one consultant familiar with

---

[4] "How to Help Your Child Become a Better Writer" (Urbana, Il.: National Council of Teachers of English), a brief pamphlet available in Spanish and English, containing simple suggestions parents can use to positively influence their children's writing.

recent work in writing than from a series of specialists, each of whom makes a presentation and then leaves your teachers to sort through the implications on their own.

Another resource for staff development in writing is available through the National Writing Project, directed by James Gray at the University of California, Berkeley. Teachers in many different parts of the country come together for a summer institute on writing at their local college or university. They share their experiences in teaching writing, learn about new approaches, and react to one another's writing. After the institute, a corps of teacher consultants is chosen from among the institute participants to carry on inservice work in local school districts during the academic year. The training the teacher consultants receive benefits their own schools as well as the schools that contract for formal inservice programs.

Administrators should recognize the special need for inservice work in the teaching of writing and provide the moral and budgetary support necessary for staff development to be a success.

Signs of Improvement

Building an effective writing program is a slow process; there is no quick cure for "the writing problem." Still, you can watch for signs of progress.

Sign 1: More evidence of writing

As you walk through your halls and visit classrooms, writing should be more evident in all subjects. Teachers will be talking with their classes about how to gather information or about how to use what is already known in writing about a particular topic. Students will be working on their own writing or discussing it with their classmates. Completed writing will be displayed in a variety of places, from bulletin boards to dittoed samplers.

Sign 2: Danger signals recede

At the same time, the "danger signals" will begin to recede. Pass rates on writing examinations should stabilize and then rise; essay items should be in greater evidence in school examinations; students who need help with their writing should have a clearly established way to get that help; and the informal comments of students and teachers should begin to shift from how bad things are toward how nicely so-and-so's work is improving.

To provide a more systematic test of your school's progress, you may want to use the following checklist. The items reflect standards for basic skills writing programs determined by a special committee of teachers, supervisors, and writing specialists for the National Council of Teachers of English and widely distributed by the Basic Skills Office of the U.S. Department of Education.

Checklist for Evaluating Writing Programs

Teaching and Learning

_____ There is evidence that knowledge of current theory and research in writing has been sought and applied in developing the writing program.

_____ Writing instruction is a substantial and clearly identified part of an integrated English language arts curriculum.

_____ Writing is called for in other subject matters across the curriculum.

_____ The subject matter of writing has its richest source in the students' personal, social, and academic interests and experiences.

_____ Students write in many forms (essays, notes, summaries, poems, letters, stories, reports, scripts, journals).

_____ Students write for a variety of audiences (to inform, to persuade, to express themselves, to explore, to clarify thinking).

_____ Class time is devoted to all aspects of the writing process: generating ideas, drafting, revising, and editing.

_____ All students receive instruction in both (a) developing and expressing ideas, and (b) using the conventions of edited American English.

_____ Control of the conventions of edited American English (supporting skills such as spelling, handwriting, punctuation, and grammatical usage) is developed primarily during the writing process and secondarily through related exercises.

_____ Students receive constructive responses—from teachers and from others—at various stages in the writing process.

Evaluation of Individual Writing Growth

_____ Is based on complete pieces of writing.

_____ Reflects informed judgments, first about clarity and content, and then about conventions of spelling, mechanics, and usage.

_____ Includes regular responses to individual pieces of student writing as well as periodic assessment measuring growth over a period of time.

Support

_____ Teachers with major responsibility for writing instruction receive continuing education reflecting current knowledge about the teaching of writing.

_____ Teachers of other subjects receive information and training in ways to make use of and respond to writing in their classes.

_____ Parent and community groups are informed about the writing program and about ways in which they can support it.

_____ School and class schedules provide sufficient time to assure that the writing process is thoroughly pursued.

_____ Teachers and students have access to and make regular use of a wide range of resources (library services, media, teaching materials, duplicating facilities) supplied for support of the writing program.

Program Evaluation

_____ Evaluation of the writing program focuses on pre- and post-program sampling of complete pieces of writing, using a recognized procedure (holistic rating, the Diederich scale, primary trait scoring) to arrive at reliable judgments about the quality of the program.

_____ Evaluation of the program might also include assessment of a sample of student attitudes; gathering of pertinent quantitative data (frequency of student writing, time devoted to writing activities), and observational data (evidence of prewriting activities, class anthologies, writing folders, and student writing displays).

(Adapted from "Standards for Basic Skills Writing Programs," Urbana, Il.: National Council of Teachers of English, 1979.)

Organizations That Can Help

The National Council of Teachers of English. NCTE produces a variety of resources on the teaching of writing that are listed in their annual publications catalog (available free). They also publish a series of journals that carry articles on the teaching of writing, including *English Journal* for secondary school teachers. NCTE will also provide names of people knowledgeable about the teaching of writing who might be willing to work with schools in your area. (Contact John C. Maxwell, Executive Director, 1111 Kenyon Road, Urbana, Illinois 61801.)

ERIC Clearinghouse on Reading and Communication Skills. A federally funded clearinghouse located at NCTE, ERIC/RCS can guide you to curriculum materials, research, and theory about the teaching of writing. The clearinghouse also publishes books and articles on the teaching of writing in conjunction with professional organizations such as NCTE. (Contact ERIC/RCS, 1111 Kenyon Road, Urbana, Illinois 61801.)

National Writing Project. The National Writing Project coordinates inservice work at a variety of sites through the United States. The director's office can direct you to the nearest writing project offering summer institutes and inservice programs. (Contact James Gray, Director, Tolman Hall, University of California-Berkeley, Berkeley, California 94720.)

National Assessment of Educational Progress. NAEP has published a series of national reports on writing achievement at various age levels. Items from the assessment can be adapted for school use. Write for current publications list. (Contact NAEP, Education Commission of the States, 1860 Lincoln Street, Denver, Colorado 80203.)

Resources for Improving Writing Programs

Applebee, Arthur N. *Writing in the Secondary School: English and the Content Areas.* Urbana, Il.: National Council of Teachers of English, 1981. Reports on the uses of writing in the major subject areas in American schools; includes a lengthy bibliography of materials suggesting practical ways to use writing in a variety of subject areas.

Cooper, Charles, and Odell, Lee, eds. *Evaluating Writing.* Urbana, Il.: National Council of Teachers of English, 1975. State-of-the-art summary of approaches to writing assessment.

Fadiman, Clifton, and Howard, James. *Empty Pages.* Washington, D.C.: Council for Basic Education, 1979. Slightly polemical overview of the writing problem and current efforts to overcome it.

Fillion, Bryant. "Language Across the Curriculum." *McGill Journal of Education* 14 (Winter 1979): 47-60. Describes three simple surveys of the writing students are doing in individual schools.

Martin, Nancy, and others. *Writing and Learning Across the Curriculum, 11-16.* London: Ward Lock, 1976. Available in the U.S. from Boynton/Cook Publishers. Useful descriptions of how writing can function in a variety of subject areas.

Myers, Miles. *A Procedure for Writing Assessment and Holistic Scoring.* Urbana, Il.: National Council of Teachers of English, 1980. Step-by-step instructions for planning, implementing, and reporting the results of systematic school or district writing assessments.

6.

Mathematics
B. Ross Taylor

The Critical Issues

What are the basic mathematical skills?

As a result of detailed surveys, the National Council of Teachers of Mathematics (NCTM) has prepared a set of Recommendations for School Mathematics in the 1980s.[1] The first of the eight major recommendations states that problem solving should be the focus of school mathematics. The second recommendation states that basic skills in mathematics should be defined to encompass more than computational facility. Specifically, NCTM recommends that the full scope of what is basic should include at least the following ten basic skills areas, as identified by the National Council of Supervisors in Mathematics in its *Position Paper on Basic Mathematical Skills:*

1. Problem solving
2. Applying mathematics to everyday situations
3. Alertness to reasonableness of results
4. Estimation and approximation
5. Appropriate computational skills
6. Geometry
7. Measurement

---

[1] The National Council of Teachers of Mathematics established the Priorities in School Mathematics Project (PRISM) to conduct surveys concerning possible mathematics curriculum changes during the 1980s. A copy of the Executive Summary of the PRISM project, as well as the booklet, *An Agenda for Action: Recommendations For School Mathematics of the 1980s* ($1.00), may be obtained from NCTM, 1906 Association Drive, Reston, Virginia 22091.

8. Tables, charts, and graphs
9. Using mathematics to predict
10. Computer literacy.[2]

Note: computation is just one of ten skills areas; to be useful, computation must be combined effectively with the other skills.

The mathematics education profession is united in support of this broad definition of basic mathematical skills. Indeed, 18 national professional organizations have endorsed the broad view in a statement of the Essentials of Education.[3]

How much mathematics should be required for graduation from high school?

NCTM recommends that at least three years of mathematics be required in grades nine through 12. Today, at least three years of college preparatory mathematics are required as prerequisites for most college majors, and four years for majors in science, mathematics, and engineering. Moreover, there is an increasing need for all students to have mathematical skills for careers and participation in modern society. However, many high schools do not require any mathematics beyond the ninth grade. Clearly there is a need for these schools to re-examine their mathematics graduation requirements.

In recent years, many states and local school districts have adopted minimum competency requirements for graduation. Usually, remedial instruction is provided to help students meet those requirements. Rather than a minimum competency requirement, however, NCTM recommends a flexible curriculum with a wide range of options to accommodate the diverse needs of the student population.

Is achievement in mathematics declining?

During the period 1967 to 1979, Scholastic Aptitude Test (SAT) mathematics scores declined from 492 to 467.[4] On national assessment

---

[2] For a copy of the *Position Paper on Basic Mathematical Skills,* send a stamped, self-addressed envelope to Ross Taylor, NCSM Basic Skills, Minneapolis Public Schools, 807 Broadway Northeast, Minneapolis, Minnesota 55413.

[3] The statement on the Essentials of Education is available from Organizations for the Essentials of Education, 1111 Kenyon Road, Urbana, Illinois 61801.

[4] The Science Education Databook, publication SE80-3 of the National Science Foundation, contains a wealth of national achievement data in science and math. Available from the Science Education Directorate, National Science Foundation, Washington, D.C. 20550.

tests in 1973 and 1978, achievement of 17-year-olds in computation with whole numbers was generally high and changed little. However, problem solving decreased about 8 percentage points.[5] In view of these results, the NCTM recommendation that problem solving be the focus of school mathematics in the 80s is particularly timely.

On national assessment tests in disadvantaged urban areas, achievement of 17-year-olds increased. Perhaps the existence of Title I and other compensatory basic skills programs at the elementary level and the absence of such programs at the secondary level can help explain these trends.

How well do females and minorities achieve in mathematics?

Achievement of boys and girls in mathematics is approximately the same through junior high school, according to information from the National Assessment of Educational Progress (NAEP) and other sources. However, males perform better than females on the SAT, and male 17-year-olds perform better than females on National Assessment tests. Avoidance of secondary school mathematics courses by females appears to be a major cause of this difference.

Results from NAEP indicate that in both 1973 and 1978 mathematics achievement of blacks and Hispanics was below achievement of whites and that the gap was wider for older students. No National Assessment information on other minorities is available. Factors that appear to contribute to the achievement gap are avoidance of secondary mathematics courses by minorities, and the dearth of compensatory basic skills programs at the secondary school level.

How well prepared are teachers in mathematics?

The subject matter knowledge of certified mathematics teachers does not appear to be a problem. Most math teachers are able to provide suitable instruction for motivated students in college preparatory mathematics courses. On the other hand, most secondary school mathematics teachers do not have specific background for teaching basic mathematical skills to low-achieving students who lack motivation and have reading difficulties as well. There is an apparent need for staff development to help teachers meet the needs of these students.

---

[5] Reports on mathematics achievement on National Assessment tests can be purchased from National Assessment of Educational Progress, 1860 Lincoln Street, Suite 300, Denver, Colorado 80295.

Data from a number of sources indicate a growing shortage of certified mathematics teachers, a shortage already severe in some parts of the country. Today mathematics teachers and college students who are strong in math are being attracted to industry. If this trend continues, the quality of mathematics instruction will suffer.

What is the impact of technology?

One of NCTM's major recommendations is that mathematics programs should take full advantage of the power of calculators and computers. Since 1975, approximately 100 research studies have investigated the impact of computers on mathematics achievement.[6] The evidence is overwhelming that the use of calculators helps, rather than hurts, learning. In all but a few cases, achievement was as high or higher when calculators were used in instruction (but not on tests).

Computer literacy is one of the ten basic skills areas specified in the National Council of Supervisors of Mathematics position paper. A recent study by the National Center for Education Statistics found that about half of the secondary schools in the nation have at least one microcomputer or terminal for instructional use by students.[7] All students should have hands-on experience with computers, which can be used effectively to enhance instruction through problem solving, classroom demonstration, and drill and practice.

Advances in electronic technology lead to changing priorities in mathematics instruction. Skills like estimation and approximation need more emphasis. Long, involved calculations will be done electronically, but computation is still important, and the ability to do rapid calculation is more important than ever.

How important is basic mathematical skill instruction?

The impact of new technology on society has increased the need for mathematics. The public is aware of this need, as evidenced in the 1979 Gallup Poll on education. Mathematics topped the list of essential subjects, with 97 percent of the respondents indicating that it is essential. Concerns over declining test scores, attention in the media, and public pressure for accountability have produced demands for programs to address competency in mathematics and the other basic skill areas.

---

[6] Information on the calculator studies is available from the Calculator Information Center, Room 201, 1200 Chambers Road, Columbus, Ohio 43212.

[7] For more information about computers in the schools, contact the National Center for Education Statistics, Room 620, Presidential Building, 6525 Belcrest Road, Hyattsville, Maryland 20782.

What programs and practices are effective?

At the national level, there has been a significant absence of secondary school programs in basic mathematical skills. For example, there are no nationally validated programs for basic mathematical skills in grades nine through 12. The National Science Foundation has concentrated its efforts in college preparatory instruction, and only very recently has the Department of Education started to focus on basic mathematical skills at the secondary school level.

In light of these considerations, it is very difficult to identify outstanding secondary school programs in basic mathematical skills. Nevertheless, on the basis of research and experience, it is possible to identify a number of promising practices.[8] The Association for Supervision and Curriculum Development has produced a videotape summarizing factors that research has shown contribute to effective instruction in basic skills.[9] The questions and discussions that follow address this issue.

Questions Principals Should Ask

Has achievement in basic mathematical skills been established as a school priority?

School leadership is critical to improving instruction. Basic skills programs have a much better chance of success when basic skills instruction is given a priority commitment by the principal.

Have the necessary resources been allocated to basic skills instruction?

A goal that establishes a priority for basic skills instruction is meaningless unless it is accompanied by a priority allocation of human and financial resources. If the goal is set by the state, the state can help implement it by providing funding to address the goal. When the local school board or central administration adopts the goal, it provides a rationale for priority allocation of staff and funds. Resources may be allocated at the district level, or the central administration can provide guidelines for principals to give priority to the allocation of building resources for basic skills

---

[8] See, for instance, Penelope L. Peterson and Herbert J. Welberg, *Research on Teaching: Concepts, Findings, and Implications* (Berkeley, Calif.: McCutchan, 1979).

[9] The 21-minute videotape, *Teacher and School Effectiveness,* features Ronald Edmonds, Barak Rosenshine, and Peter Mortimore. Available for rent or purchase from ASCD, 225 N. Washington Street, Alexandria, Virginia 22314.

instruction. Such guidelines help keep "peace in the family" when the basic skills receive a high proportion of the school's limited resources.

Are course requirements in mathematics sufficient for graduation?

NCTM recommends that any school requiring less than three years of mathematics in grades nine through 12 consider re-examining their graduation requirements. Every school's programs should give students the background they will need in modern society.

What is the present status of enrollment in mathematics?

There are a number of things to look for in enrollment data. What proportion of students are taking only the minimum course requirements in math? At what levels do students tend to stop taking mathematics? Do girls, Hispanics, blacks, or American Indians tend to avoid mathematics? Information on assessing enrollment in mathematics and increasing the enrollment of underrepresented groups is available from NCTM.[10]

Are students informed about mathematics and their future?

According to a recent national study, the most important factor influencing participation in mathematics is knowledge of how useful mathematics will be.[11] Mathematics teachers and counselors should make a concerted effort to see that students receive information about the high school mathematics courses they will need for careers and higher education. Career information brochures and posters are available from NCTM[12] and from the Minneapolis Public Schools,[13] which has prepared a series for each high school course.

---

[10] A series of videotapes for students, teachers, parents, and counselors, entitled *Multiplying Options and Subtracting Bias,* has been developed under the direction of Elizabeth Fennema. The videotapes and supporting materials are available for purchase or rent from NCTM, 1906 Association Drive, Reston, Virginia 22091.

[11] Jane Armstrong and Stuart Kahl, *An Overview of Factors Affecting Women's Participation in Mathematics* (Denver: NAEP, 1979). For a report of the study, write to the National Assessment of Educational Progress, 1860 Lincoln Street, Suite 700, Denver, Colorado 80295.

[12] The series of color posters and accompanying brochures may be purchased from NCTM, 1906 Association Drive, Reston, Virginia 22091.

[13] A poster and brochures are available at nominal cost from the Minneapolis Mathematics Club, 807 Broadway Northeast, Minneapolis, Minnesota 55413.

What is the present status of achievement in mathematics?

A first step is to obtain existing information, particularly information that has already been compiled or is easily obtainable. Many secondary schools do not have much data available concerning achievement in basic mathematical skills. Thus, the key question to ask is whether you are able to identify students with needs in basic math skills, provide them with instruction in those skills, and determine the extent to which they master the skills. Depending on the answer to this question, some additional testing may be needed. If it is, great care must be taken in selecting the test, for it will strongly influence the direction of the program. Initial baseline test data is useful when implementing a new program; it can help in determining what change has occurred and in identifying weaknesses in the curriculum.

How should the issue of minimum competency in mathematics for graduation be handled?

Since 1975, many states and individual school districts have mandated competency requirements. In those cases, individual schools do not have the freedom to decide if there should be such a requirement, but they may have some choice as to how the requirement should be implemented.

On the one hand, there are a number of problems associated with a minimum competency requirement. On the other hand, the needs of many students may be ignored in the absence of such a requirement. The Racine, Wisconsin, Public Schools have taken the middle ground; competency seals are affixed to diplomas of students who achieve particular competency levels in mathematics and several other subject areas.

Has mathematics curriculum leadership been identified, developed, and supported?

Usually, the mathematics department chairperson is responsible for providing leadership for the mathematics program. The chairperson should be supported by release time or extra remuneration. The chairperson should be an individual who demonstrates leadership and organizational skills, has a knowledge of mathematics education, and has the confidence of the department. The principal can also create a climate to draw out initiative and leadership from all teachers. Mathematics teachers should be encouraged to participate in activities of NCTM and its affiliated regional, state, and local professional mathematics education organizations.

In schools where the chairperson serves as a department head with supervisory responsibilities, he or she can benefit from becoming active in the National Council of Supervisors of Mathematics. In school systems large enough to have mathematics supervisors, principals can seek out and fully utilize the services of the supervisor.

Are there objectives with tests to match?

Basic skills objectives should not be limited to computation. They should address the ten basic skill areas defined in NCSM's *Position Paper on Basic Mathematical Skills*. Initially, objectives can be selected or developed by a small task force of teachers, possibly with some external support from mathematics education specialists. The state mathematics supervisor can be contacted to ensure that local objectives are in line with state objectives or guidelines. The objectives should be reviewed by teachers and, possibly, by administrators, parents, students, and the community. This process will both improve the objectives and build ownership. The objectives should be finalized on the basis of information from the review. If each objective is accompanied by a sample test item, everyone will have a clearer idea of the meaning of the objective.

Standardized norm-referenced tests are usually not suitable for secondary school basic skills programs because they do not match the objectives of the program. Criterion-referenced tests are more suitable because they can be designed to measure achievement of the objectives of the program and to diagnose individual needs for monitoring student progress and providing information for program evaluation.

Is instruction in basic mathematical skills systematic?

A systematic program of instruction begins with a clear set of objectives and a testing program to match. It should have a means of identifying students who are not achieving up to expectations and students who are achieving well above expectations. It should help identify specific learning needs and provide teachers with information that can help organize students and staff for instruction.

A systematic program also helps teachers organize learning materials to address specific objectives. Instruction for individual students and groups of students should be modified on the basis of feedback information from testing and teacher observation. Item analysis information from the testing program can be used to identify and remedy weak spots in the curriculum. Successful schools and programs should be identified and their essential ideas replicated whenever possible. Test results should be returned as rapidly as they are needed.

Are there provisions for maintenance of previously learned skills?

In Minneapolis we have consistently found that achievement increases substantially whenever a skill maintenance program is implemented. This should not be surprising since it is much easier to stop students from forgetting than it is to teach them in the first place.

Generally, in a skills maintenance program, students have a 5- to 15-minute period of systematic review every day or every other day. Skills maintenance should include opportunities for following up on weaknesses and for practicing test-taking skills. A skills maintenance system is relatively easy to develop and implement, and it probably will have a greater impact on improving test scores than anything else you will do.

Are there provisions for the development of a curriculum that addresses the objectives?

The selection of the objectives and tests and the implementation of a systematic approach to instruction are part of the curriculum development process. With clear objectives and a testing program to match, the school is in a position to implement a systematic approach to curriculum development. Weaknesses can be identified and priorities established on the basis of sound, relevant information. In addition to item analysis information from test results, data should be received from teachers, teacher aides, parents, and, in some cases, students. Also, input should be obtained from professional meetings, literature, and professional contacts. Investigations should be made to find out what has worked in other locations. Information from publishers should be sought. Wherever possible, existing materials should be used or adapted. If no suitable existing materials are found, then new materials need to be developed, piloted, and revised as necessary on the basis of results of the pilot.

Are calculators and computers being used in mathematics instruction?

Students will live in a world where calculators and computers are readily accessible. If they haven't mastered computation by the time they reach secondary school, they might be better served by emphasizing problem solving with the help of a calculator than by continuing to hammer away at paper-and-pencil algorithms such as long division. Students should also get hands-on experience with computers, which should have more scope than the standard computer drill and practice routines.

Is there adequate funding for learning materials for basic mathematics courses?

Basic skills courses tend to use far more in the way of consumable learning materials than college preparatory courses. Furthermore, basic skills students can benefit especially from hands-on experiences with "concrete" learning materials. They should have access to calculators and computers for computer-assisted instruction. Special extra funding may be necessary for learning materials and equipment for basic skills courses.

Is instruction in basic mathematical skills geared to the abilities of the students?

In secondary basic skills classes, particular attention must be paid to prerequisite skills. Basic skills students need successful learning experiences. They must receive instruction in areas where they have the necessary prerequisite background.

There is a considerable body of evidence that hands-on experiences with manipulative materials are effective for learning mathematics concepts. Manipulative materials tend to be used more at the elementary school level, while secondary school teachers are usually more paper-and-pencil oriented. Nevertheless, many secondary school students are at a cognitive level where they need concrete experiences in order to learn mathematical concepts. The idea is to find concrete experiences that are both meaningful and motivating.

Is instruction in basic mathematical skills geared to the interests of the students?

Students tend to prefer problems and applications that relate to their current activities or have recreational appeal. After eight or nine unsuccessful years of taking mathematics, a year of remedial arithmetic may not be all that exciting. Vocational mathematics tends to have appeal only after the student has made a commitment to the vocation. Mathematics problems that machinists encounter have little appeal to students who do not plan a career in that area. Consumer mathematics tends to appeal more to juniors and seniors than to freshmen and sophomores. Programs that focus on solving problems that are interesting to the students appear to show promise.

Students enrolled in basic skills courses often have poor attendance patterns. In effect, the dropout is society's problem, but the "drop-in" (who drops in to class every now and then) is the school's problem.

Between the drop-in problem, the high mobility rate of many basic skills students, and the lack of prerequisite skills of many students, a degree of individualization is necessary in basic skills classes. However, research from a number of studies has indicated that the self-paced model for instruction is usually not as effective as traditional instruction. In fact, the self-paced model for individualized instruction tends to be least effective for low-achieving, poorly motivated students.[14]

Are classes free from interruption?

It is no surprise that research has shown that the amount of time spent on-task is a major factor affecting achievement. Interruptions from address system announcements, individual messages, or class dismissal for assemblies or other school activities have a negative impact on time-on-task and, hence, on achievement.

In addition, secondary mathematics basic skills classes tend to focus on students with problems in motivation, learning, and behavior. Therefore, these classes need special attention from administrators to ensure that disruptions that prevent learning do not occur. Teachers of these classes need firm support by administrators.

Are high expectations communicated and rewarded when met?

A body of evidence suggests that expectations influence achievement and become self-fulfilling prophecies. High expectations for students and staff should be communicated to the staff, the parents, and the students. In turn, teachers should communicate their high expectations for students to the students and to the parents.

If achievement is a priority, the principal should see that test scores are reviewed, to identify both problems and successes. A letter of praise from the principal can make a major contribution to even greater success. Likewise, when students receive positive reinforcement from teachers, their achievement is favorably affected. Immediate feedback motivates further learning.

When parents receive timely and specific information on student achievement, they can also provide praise, or intervention, if needed.

---

[14] For a summary of the research, see Harold L. Schoen, "Implications of Research for Instruction in Self-paced Mathematics Classrooms" in *Organizing for Mathematics* (Reston, Va.: National Council of Teachers of Mathematics, 1977).

Does the principal communicate effectively about the basic skills program?

Principals should maintain open channels of communication with the mathematics staff about the basic skills program. They should visit classes and meet with mathematics teachers and the department chairperson to communicate expectations and review progress. The principal should be available to the chairperson and the teachers for consultation. Teachers should receive positive reinforcement both verbally and in writing. The principal should communicate the priority for basic skills instruction to the students, the entire faculty, and the community, by speaking at meetings and by writing in school publications.

Is the student/teacher ratio appropriate?

The normal ratio of approximately 30 students to one teacher is suitable for college preparatory mathematics courses. However, many students who enroll in basic skills courses have poor motivation, low reading skills, weak mathematics background, numerous learning difficulties, and behavior problems. To compensate for these difficulties, class size should be kept small (15 to 20 students). Where possible, adult or student aides should be provided.

Do teachers have the qualifications and the commitment?

For basic mathematical skills instruction to succeed, teachers must be prepared for and committed to teaching basic mathematical skills. All too often, mathematics teachers do not prefer to teach basic skills courses, which, as a result, are often taught by teachers lowest in the "pecking order" (with the least seniority), or farmed out to teachers in other departments. This process can result in a high turnover of teachers in basic skills courses, or courses taught by teachers who do not place a high priority on basic mathematical skills instruction.

The principal should discontinue assignment of classes by seniority, and balance the assignment of classes so that teachers of "preferred" classes also teach some basic skills classes. When new mathematics teachers are hired, priority should be given to teachers who have particular interest and expertise in teaching basic skills. Basic skills courses should be taught by mathematics teachers, not by teachers in other departments to fill out their schedules.

Special supervisory attention to mathematics classes is likely to result in clearly measurable gains in achievement. ASCD has available two videotapes on evaluating teacher performance, which administrators can use to improve their supervision skills.[15]

Are there provisions for staff development?

Mathematics teachers tend to be strong in their knowledge of mathematics, but they frequently lack knowledge of how to teach poorly motivated students who have not yet mastered basic mathematical skills. Mathematics teachers also need to learn about interrelationships between reading, oral language proficiency, and the learning of mathematics.[16] They need relevant and practical staff development. School systems with mathematics supervisors should look to them for staff development. Nearby colleges and universities may offer needed course work, or college faculty members can be brought in to lead inservice activities. The state mathematics supervisor should have information on staff development opportunities in the state. Teachers of basic skills courses should be given priority for staff development opportunities, provided with financial support, and given release time to attend meetings of the National Council of Teachers of Mathematics and its affiliated state and local organizations. This will give them the chance to pick up valuable ideas which can be passed to other teachers in inservice. Support for attendance at professional meetings contributes to the notion that basic skills courses are prestige courses to teach.

Is there sufficient planning for continuous success of new programs?

A new or revised basic skills program may be piloted in one or more classes or implemented across the board. The program should be carefully monitored and evaluated and changes made as necessary. It is a good idea to start a program with a low profile and then give it publicity after it becomes successful.

Sometimes special external funding is needed to develop and implement new programs. Whenever special funding is used for program change, care should be taken to see that the ongoing program does not depend on the special funding. There should be sufficient "hard money" to main-

---

[15] *Evaluating Teacher Performance,* featuring Richard Manatt. Available from the Association for Supervision and Curriculum Development, 225 N. Washington Street, Alexandria, Virginia 22314.

[16] The International Reading Association has reading aids series, which includes *Teaching Reading and Mathematics* by Richard A. Earle. For information, contact The International Reading Association, Newark, Delaware 19711.

tain the program when the "soft money" used to initiate the program is no longer available.

If your staff plans carefully, has high expectations, and makes needed changes as it goes along, the program is likely to be successful.

7.

A Thematic Interdisciplinary Approach to Basic Skills in the Secondary School

M. Jerry Weiss

The key person in an interdisciplinary approach to basic skills instruction is the reading teacher. Since the ability to read and comprehend subject matter is so vital to achievement in all content areas, the reading teacher can do much to help teachers in every department promote student success.

Initiating an Interdisciplinary Unit

The Reading Committee

The first step in developing a thematic interdisciplinary program is to form a reading committee comprised of interested volunteers. The committee should be chaired by the reading teacher or reading specialist and include representatives from each department, the library staff, and guidance services, as well as an administrator with the authority to make schoolwide decisions and take actions.

The committee's purpose is to reach definite conclusions about the function of the reading instruction in the school. It considers what shall be taught, when, by whom, with what materials, and how different departments can reinforce each other's efforts. The reading teacher raises questions the committee needs to consider before making recommendations. The reading chair also suggests methods and materials that will allow more students to succeed through joint teaching efforts, rather than through one person's efforts in a reading laboratory or center. Since each person on the committee contributes to reading instruction, the reading teacher can help committee members understand the role each department and each special service plays in meeting students' reading needs.

Committee meetings need to focus on the following key topics:

1. Formal and informal diagnostic techniques—ways to find out what hinders and what helps student progress.

2. Design and effective use of interest and experience inventories for each discipline so that classroom teachers will receive appropriate background information about students.

3. Realistic goals for mastery of content—objectives based on the understanding that a variety of skill levels are present in a single classroom.

4. Skills necessary to meet the goals—reading, writing, listening, speaking, and viewing skills.

5. Resources needed to complete assignments—print and nonprint.

6. Motivational and project activities that will stimulate and maintain student interest.

7. Suggestions for teaching the skills—use of worksheets developed by the teacher, or commercial resources and games; the effective use of media, lectures, and demonstrations; problem-solving activities that require students to identify, learn, and apply skills.

8. Suggestions for evaluating student progress—teacher-made tests related to the specific skills and objectives to be mastered; daily observations of students while they work on assignments; student participation in class discussions; quantity and quality of materials used to fulfill assignments; students' ability to transfer skills and ideas to a variety of situations; students' development of characteristics such as dependability, initiative, promptness, independence, cooperation, organization, articulation, resourcefulness.

Other matters may arise at the committee meetings, but these need to be explored in depth. Recordkeeping, homework assignments, and teacher-student conferences are also important in helping teachers develop management procedures for working with students and meeting special individual and group needs.

Members of the committee should take the minutes of each meeting to their respective departments for discussion and to obtain feedback. It is important that the total faculty get a feeling for the concerns and deliberations of the committee. Excellent questions may arise during a department meeting that should be discussed during a reading committee meeting as well. This arrangement fosters an inservice program that starts with the committee and spreads to all staff members.

Once enough recommendations have been made, the committee can request a pilot program to initiate a thematic unit taught by an interdisciplinary team. That team should consist of four or five teachers from different departments who share the same 100 or so students.

Scheduling for Team Teaching

Scheduling is important, both for the teachers and the students. Team members should have a common preparation period each day. A schedule such as the one below facilitates planning; teachers can use the preparation period to meet with each other or with small groups of students, or to develop their individual lesson plans. During the same block of time, students should be scheduled for gym classes, electives, or study hall—classes they can afford to be taken out of if they need special help or the opportunity to work on projects in the thematic basic skills program.

Figure 1. Teacher Schedule

Teacher and Subject	Period 1	Period 2	Period 3	Period 4	Period 5	Period 6	Period 7
Adams (English)	8^1	8^2	8^3	8^4	lunch	8^5	preparation
Baker (S. Stud.)	8^2	8^3	8^4	8^5	lunch	8^1	preparation
Carney (Math)	8^3	8^4	8^5	lunch	8^1	8^2	preparation
Dale (Science)	8^4	8^5	8^1	lunch	8^2	8^3	preparation
Edwards (Music)	8^5	8^1	8^2	lunch	8^3	8^4	preparation

Using this schedule, students are heterogeneously grouped in classes of 20 to 25 per period. When initiating the program, it is best to have fewer students in each section to give teachers enough time to acclimate themselves to the new procedures. They must learn to plan together, to cooperate, to discuss ways for using blocks of time with ease and flexibility.

For example, if the English teacher wants to show a full-length movie about the topic being developed, he or she can show the complete movie in one day to all of the students. The other teachers can watch the movie and draw examples that apply to their own subjects. Or, if the science teacher needs to keep some students for a double period, the other teachers on the team can adjust their instructional plans accordingly. This back-to-back scheduling allows more effective use of teachers' and students' time. Certain lessons should not be ended after 40 minutes simply because the bell rings; learning does not necessarily revolve around such a time sequence.

The teachers who are selected for the pilot project should be given time for inservice. They should be compatible and sensitive to the needs and interests of students. They should also understand the importance of reinforcing each other's efforts and standards.

Students should be made aware of those standards from the start. For instance, rules for completing assignments should be posted on bulletin boards—not to be looked at and forgotten, but to be reinforced by the teacher, who should make his or her expectations known to the students.

The Reading Teacher's Role

Once the pilot program has begun, the reading teacher's role is to work with teachers in their classrooms. As the theme unit is developed and implemented, the reading teacher helps identify necessary skills for successful mastery of the subject, and suggests materials and methods useful for teaching the students these skills within the context of the unit. At times, a reading teacher can work with groups of students in the cluster who need help with specific skills.

The major function of the reading teacher is to help classroom teachers assume more responsibility for and confidence in teaching reading skills in the content areas. In many secondary schools, students are pulled out of classrooms and assigned to a reading center for special help. Not many schools organize skill instruction in coordination with specific content area needs or provide a successful transfer of skills learned in laboratories and centers to the regular classroom. In contrast, the thematic unit plans with cluster teaching offer a wide range of reading materials for all students to use. Teachers work together to help students master concepts and skills from discipline to discipline.

The mastery and application of basic skills and the development of a positive attitude occur when students are surrounded by a variety of books on many subjects and when they experience a variety of approaches to learning.

Among the topics that have been used successfully as interdisciplinary themes are (1) consumerism, (2) running the country, (3) cities and urban life, (4) other countries and tourism, (5) conflicts and resolutions, (6) a world after the last war, and (7) growing with healthy minds and bodies. All five disciplines cut across all of these themes.

What follows is a description of a sample unit adapted to the thematic, interdisciplinary approach. The theme of this unit is communications.

Sample Unit:
Introduction to the World of Communications

Concepts

The major forms of communication to be studied during the next six to eight weeks are (1) music and art, (2) radio and television, (3) film, (4) the press, and (5) theater and dance.

Students will be grouped according to their interest in studying *one* of the five subgroups listed above. (If a student chooses the first area, he or she will work in both art and music.)

Some key topics to be developed: (1) Who are/were some of the major personalities identified with this field of communications? (2) How has technology changed or contributed to the development of communications, particularly the area you are studying? (3) What talents and resources are needed in each area? (4) How have the developments and changes within the communications field affected social customs and lifestyles? (5) What educational experiences are suggested for a better understanding of the communications world and the future of this field? (6) What careers are possible for people interested in a particular field of communications?

Suggestions for Areas for Skill Development

1. Reading

• Specialized vocabulary—symbols, manual dexterity, perception, tone, inflection, harmony, rhythmn, texture, color, aesthetics, imagery, soundtrack, settings, patterns, verbal, nonverbal, form, intuition, visual literacy, tactile, auditory, sound waves, light waves, mass media, gold record, satellite, zoom, microphone, situation comedy, soap opera, documentary, jazz, concerto, symphony, opera, ballet, modern dance, choreograph, edit, blues, soul, country-western, classical, syndication, comedy, tragedy, farce, "ratings," connotation, denotation, semantics, linguistics, interview, columnist, producer, director, press agency, photographer, gesture, mime, sign language, body language, makeup, lay out, musical score, costumes, sound effects, script, cue, screening, show format, marketing and sales, promotional tour, transmit, stage directions, casting, staging, tape playback, countdown, engineer, special effects, "Grammy," "Emmy," "Oscar," "Tony," timing, technical crew, ADI (areas of dominant influence), spot announcements, props, RPM, adaptations.

- Use of reference materials
- Reading diagrams, charts, tables, maps
- Reading and interpreting scripts
- Following directions
- Understanding a time line
- Sequencing
- Seeing a cause-effect relationship
- Understanding propaganda devices
- Skimming for pertinent information
- Outlining
- Note-taking
- Interpreting visual symbols
- Interpreting body movements

2. Writing

- Research techniques and reports
- A variety of newspaper stories—feature articles, interviews, news stories, advertisements, editorials
- Writing and interpretation of a statistical survey
- Playwriting (for stage, radio, film, or television)
- Photo-essays
- Writing and illustrating books or magazine articles
- Cartooning, including drawing and captioning
- Writing headlines
- Writing poems, songs, or short stories

3. Listening

- To recordings, dramatic and musical
- To stories told by classmates, teachers, special guests
- To sound effects as part of laboratory experience in sound identification

4. Speaking

- Oral reports
- Participation in dramatic activities
- Class discussions
- Panel and forum presentations
- Persuasive argumentation (selling, advertising, promotional efforts)
- Effective use of propaganda techniques
- Sing-alongs including parodies and original songs as well as a variety of types of songs—hymns, folk songs, gospels, popular songs, musical theatre songs, and semi-classical songs

5. Viewing

- Art exhibits and displays
- Film techniques and reviewing
- Television programming and reviewing
- Filmstrips
- Photographs
- Book and magazine illustrations
- Advertisements

6. Mathematics

- Have students count the number of commercials shown on one channel between 8:00 p.m. and 10:00 p.m. each weekday night.
- Find the cost of each commercial and calculate how much money the station made during five days.
- Have the students figure out the number of column inches in one daily newspaper devoted to international and national news, regional and local news, obituaries, sports, entertainment, department store advertisements, grocery store advertisements.
- Determine what percentage of the paper contains advertisements and what percentage contains news, including editorials, feature columns, syndicated columns, and comics.
- Divide the class into groups of four. Each group has $2 million to promote a new product or special event. Have each group use advertising rate cards for radio, television, newspapers, and magazines to plan the advertising campaign within the budget. (Students interested in art or music or journalism, should try developing the actual ad programs.)
- Have each student use a major weekly magazine to determine the amount of advertising in a single issue.
- Problem: A student has been selected to be a disc jockey for a local radio station. The DJ is on from 3:00 p.m. to 6:00 p.m. Fifty 20-second spot commercials must be injected during this time. Plan a program of music and commercials to fill that slot. Allow some time for patter. Students must indicate where commercials fit and the playing time for each period. List title of record, performer, and playing time for each record.

7. Some Possible Motivational Activities:

- Show the documentary film, *When Comedy Was King,* and discuss the development of film comedy from the silent days through films of the early 40s.
- Have students raise question about the field of communications in which they have the most interest.
- Give students a list of commercials, and have them identify the product associated with each commercial. (Heavenly Coffee; Fly the Friendly Skies; We Try Harder; The White Tornado; Better Things for Better Living Through Chemistry; It's the Real Thing; You Deserve a Break Today; Take the Bus and Leave the Driving to Us; When It Rains, It Pours; We're Bullish on America; When You Care Enough to Send the Very Best.)
- Have each student take one new product or event and plan a total advertising campaign for it—for radio, newspaper and magazine, television, posters, bumper stickers, and buttons.

- Have students in other classes react to the advertising efforts.
- Invite a guest speaker from each of the five areas of communications to describe the activities involved in each of these areas.

Instructional Activities

The key topics listed under the category of "Concepts" will be the guiding purposes for planning instructional activities. Some key names that students should know might include: Thomas Edison, Woody Allen, David Sarnoff, Orson Welles, Helen Hayes, Billie Holiday, Leonard Bernstein, Norman Rockwell, Andrew Wyeth, G. B. Trudeau, Johnny Carson, Ed Sullivan, the Barrymore family, Jessica Tandy and Hume Cronyn, Alexander Calder, Salvador Dali, Andy Warhol, Marc Chagall, Carl Sagan, Edward R. Murrow, Dan Rather, Pauline Kael, Marshall McLuhan, James Agee, Mack Sennett, D. W. Griffith, H. L. Mencken, Alfred Hitchcock, Ingmar Bergman, Walter Kerr, Tom Wolfe, John Simon, Charles Chaplin, Kenny Rogers, Loretta Lynn, Walt Disney, Louis Armstrong, Duke Ellington, Reginald Rose, Tennessee Williams, Edward Albee, Ossie Davis, Sidney Poitier, Ruby Dee, Eugene O'Neill, Gore Vidal, Stan Kenton, Eubie Blake, Ogden Nash, Martha Graham, Bob Fosse, Michael Kidd, Hermes Pan, Fred Astaire, Jose Limon, Edward Steichen, William Randolph Hearst, Henry R. Luce, Adolph S. Ochs.

Questions students might be asked to consider include: What criteria should be used in evaluating the effectiveness of the communications processes? What factors might affect the effectiveness of any communications process? Students might also be asked to develop a publication, *Today's Communications World.* Have students from each group write articles for this new publication. Discuss what articles might appeal to potential subscribers. Develop advertising rate cards for potential advertisers.

Pictures speak louder than words. Take the following ten concepts, and have students divide into interest groups around each of these topics and develop a collage that conveys their ideas about the subject: (1) Unity in Diversity; (2) The American Dream; (3) The Power of Laughter; (4) The Values of Freedom; (5) The Importance of Creativity; (6) Justice for All; (7) The Future; (8) a Sense of Beauty; (9) The Technological Society; (10) Numbers in Our Lives.

Have students do a survey of the television shows, radio shows, or movies they listened to or watched during the past month. Prepare graphs to depict the results of each survey.

Have students attend a theatre production, a concert, or a dance presentation, and write a news article and a feature article about their experiences.

Have students visit a local radio station, television station, or newspaper plant, and have the students write a brief report of their visits.

Have students visit a museum and plan an oral and, if possible, visual presentation based on that trip.

Have students adapt a poem or short story for radio, television, film, stage, or dance.

Have students listen to an old show album, such as *Oklahoma,* and plan a modern story to accompany the music and lyrics. Have other students design sets and costumes.

Have students interview an author who lives within a reasonable distance of the school; plan the interview session as if it were to appear on television, radio, or in a magazine.

Have students working in the press area send letters to five different magazines and newspapers asking for a sample copy. At the same time, request a copy of the advertising rates for that publication and compare the costs for promoting certain products. Who pays for the advertising? How does this affect the consumers?

Have the music and art group take each of these titles and plan ways for developing interest in ten books and movies with the following titles: (1) *Ragtime;* (2) *The Comic World of Peanuts;* (3) *Stained Glass;* (4) *A Host of Ghosts;* (5) *Gone With The Wind;* (6) *Folk Songs U.S.A.;* (7) *Portrait of a Hero;* (8) *Tunnel Vision;* (9) *Bring Me Your Dreams;* (10) *Super Fantasy.*

Have each group make a scrapbook on the assigned general topic in which they collect articles and examples, and write explanations of why these are worth preserving. Complete bibliographical information should be included in the scrapbook for each article and picture.

Each student should keep a personal bibliography of all of the sources used for finding information about the assigned project. Comments on the articles and books also should be included.

Arrange a panel of students who will present different points of view on each of the following topics: "The Effects of Mass Media on Our Society"; "The Importance of the Arts in the Modern World"; "How Free Should a Free Press Be?"; "The Future of the Computer in the Communications Fields."

Grouping

Students should be grouped according to interests in the specific topics and for skills needs for completing assignments as required. In addition, students particularly talented in music, art, drama, photography, or writing should work in groups that best use their talents.

Evaluation

Each student will submit a written report to show what has been learned. (This might be part of group's report.) A bibliography of books and other materials should be included.

Each student will participate in an *oral* presentation with his or her group to share what has been learned about the area of study. Students will be evaluated on the effectiveness and accuracy of oral presentation.

All students will fill out a questionnaire to determine their attitudes toward the unit of study. (Popham has some excellent suggestions for assessing affect as a part of an evaluation process.)

All students will take a test to see how well they have met the objectives of the course. (A pretest can be given to determine what the students already know about the unit as well as to determine what skills have been mastered. The pretest also will identify a student's strengths and weaknesses in certain skill areas, and the data should be used for planning specific instructional programs.) The final test will also indicate how well basic skills related to the unit of study have been mastered.

Teachers can observe daily growth as students complete their assignments. As skills are taught, teachers can note which students have mastered the skills and can apply them and which students might need additional help or more time.

Sample Bibliography for Communications Unit

Ames, Evelyn. *A Wind From The West*. Boston: Houghton Mifflin, 1970.

Apel, Willi, and Ralph T. Daniel, eds. *The Harvard Brief Dictionary of Music*. New York: Pocket Books, 1961.

Battcock, Gregory, ed. *The New Art: A Critical Anthology*. New York: Dutton, 1973.

Bernstein, Leonard. *The Infinite Variety Of Music*. New York: Signet, 1970.

Bing, Rudolf. *5000 Nights At The Opera*. New York: Popular Library, 1973.

Casals, Pablo. *Joys And Sorrows*. New York: Simon & Schuster, 1970.

Clurman, Harold, ed. *Famous American Plays Of The 1930's*. New York: Dell, 1973.

Cohn, Nik. *Rock From The Beginning*. New York: Pocket Books, 1970.

Corrigan, Robert W., ed. *Twentieth-Century British Drama*. New York: Dell, 1965.

de Mille, Agnes. *Speak To Me, Dance With Me*. Boston: Little, Brown, 1973.

de Veaux, Alexis. *Don't Explain: A Song Of Billie Holiday*. New York: Harper & Row, 1980.

Dobbs, Stephen M., ed. *Arts Education And Back To Basics*. Reston, Va.: National Art Education Association, 1979.

Edmondson, Madeleine, and David Rounds. *The Soaps: Daytime Serials of Radio And TV*. New York: Stein & Day, 1973.

Ellington, Edward Kennedy. *Music Is My Mission*. New York: Doubleday, 1973.

Francks, Olive R., and Claire Ashby-Davis, ed. *Tapestry: The Interrelationships Of The Arts In Reading And Language Development*. Elmsford, N.Y.: Collegium Book Publishers, 1979.

Gattegno, Caleb. *Towards A Visual Culture: Educating Through Television*. New York: Avon, 1971.

Hansberry, Lorraine. *A Raisin In The Sun—The Sign In Sidney Brustein's Window*. New York: Signet, 1966.

Harris, Julie. *Julie Harris Talks To Young Actors*. New York: Lothrop, 1971.

Hearn, Michael Patrick. *The Art Of The Broadway Poster*. New York: Ballantine, 1980.

Hellman, Hal. *Communications In The World Of The Future*. New York: M. Evans, 1969.

Hellman, Lillian. *The Collected Plays*. Boston: Little, Brown, 1972.

Highman, Charles, and Joel Greenberg. *The Celluloid Muse: Hollywood Directors Speak*. New York: Signet, 1972.

Kael, Pauline. *Reeling*. New York: Warner, 1977.

Kirschner, Allen, and Linda Kirschner, ed. *Film: Readings In The Mass Media*. New York: Odyssey Press, 1971.

Kirschner, Allen, and Linda Kirschner, ed. *Radio And Television: Readings In The Mass Media*. New York: Odyssey Press, 1971.

Koch, Howard. *The Panic Broadcast: Portrait Of An Event*. Boston: Little, Brown, 1970.

Lackman, Ron. *Remember Radio*. New York: Putnam, 1970.

Lackman, Ron. *Remember Television*. New York: Putnam, 1971.

Leinwoll, Stanley. *From Spark To Satellite: A History Of Radio Communication*. New York: Scribners, 1979.

Mayer, Martin. *About Television*. New York: Harper & Row, 1972.

McCabe, Peter, and Robert D. Schonfeld. *Apple To The Core: The Unmasking Of The Beatles*. New York: Pocket Books, 1972.

Mersand, Joseph, ed. *Three Dramas Of American Realism*. New York: Washington Square Press, 1961.

Miller, Jim, ed. *The Rolling Stone Illustrated History Of Rock And Roll*. New York: Random House, 1980.

Monaco, James. *How To Read A Film*. New York: Oxford, 1977.

Morse, David, ed. *Grandfather Rock*. New York: Dell, 1973.

Newman, Edwin. *Strictly Speaking*. Indianapolis: Bobbs-Merrill, 1974.

Newmeyer, Sarah. *Enjoying Modern Art*. New York: Signet, 1957.

Olfson, Lewy, editor. *50 Great Scenes For Student Actors*. New York: Bantam, 1972.

Pleasants, Henry. *Serious Music—And All That Jazz!* New York: Simon & Schuster, 1971.

Quick, John. *Artists' And Illustrators' Encyclopedia*. New York: McGraw-Hill, 1969.

Richards, Stanly, editor. *Ten Great Musicals Of The American Theatre*. Radnor, Pa.: Chilton, 1973.

Robinson, Jerry. *The Comics: An Illustrated History Of Seventy-Five Years Of Comic Strip Art*. New York: Putnam, 1974.

Robinson, Richard. *Electric Rock*. New York: Pyramid, 1971.

Robinson, Richard. *Pop, Rock And Soul*. New York: Pyramid, 1972.

Rolling Stone Magazine Editors. *Knockin' On Dylan's Door: On The Road In '74*. New York: Pocket Books, 1974.

Sarlin, Bob. *Turn It Up! (I Can't Hear The Words)*. New York: Simon & Schuster, 1974.

Schicke, C.A. *Revolution In Sound*. Boston: Little, Brown, 1974.

Shestack, Melvin, ed. *The Country Music Encyclopedia*. New York: Crowell, 1974.

Stedman, Raymond William. *The Serials: Suspense And Drama By Installment*. Norman, Okla.: University of Oklahoma Press, 1971.

Turner, Darwin T., ed. *Black Drama In America: An Anthology*. New York: Fawcett, 1973.

Valdes, Joan, and Jeanne Crow, ed. *The Media Reader*. Cincinnati: Pflaum-Standard, 1973.

Wood, Michael. *Amercia In The Movies*. New York: Basic Books, 1975.

Woodyard, George, ed. *The Modern Stage In Latin America: Six Plays*. New York: Dutton, 1971.

Schrank, Jeffrey. *Understanding Mass Media*. Skokie, Ill.: National Textbook Co., 1975.

In addition to the books mentioned above, many publications such as *TV Guide, Modern Screen, Film Comment, Variety,* and major reference materials can be used to meet the needs of the students who are fulfilling the requirements of the unit.

Films, filmstrips, records, slides, art reproductions, and so forth, will be constantly used by various groups and by the entire class. Students will be asked to watch certain television programs or to listen to certain radio programs as the unit gets underway. These resources, which add variety through multimedia experiences, are readily available in many homes and libraries.

8.

Instructional Materials: Avoiding the Perils of Mix and Match

Elaine Lindheim

The concept of "mix and match" may not be an American invention, but the practice ranks high as a national institution. The idea is quite simple. Just begin with a few standard, interchangeable parts, add several options, and let free choice prevail. We have mix-and-match wardrobes (ten different outfits from the same four garments), mix-and-match vacations (stop at as many cities as you'd like for the same roundtrip fare), and mix-and-match diet plans (select two fruits from List A and three vegetables from List B). A fast food franchise has made its fortune by finetuning mix-and-match so that each of us can "have it our way." On the West Coast, where instability and earthquakes are both facts of life, there are even mix-and-match dating services—companies that specialize in all sorts of unusual pairings. In secondary schools, electives provide students with mix-and-match options. Many high schools offer alternative ways to earn a high school diploma in another version of the mix-and-match game.

Materials Mix and Match

There is one important educational area, however, where mixing and matching is not practical. That area is the selection of teaching materials to use in implementing skills-based instructional programs. Suppose, for example, that your school is about to institute a basic skills instructional program. Perhaps your district or the state requires students to pass a proficiency examination in order to graduate. Each school has been directed to design one or more instructional programs to prepare students for the competency test. If staff members are permitted to take a mix-and-match approach to selecting instructional materials associated with their programs, or if they are permitted to choose from a wide range of "somewhat related" materials in a well-meaning attempt to provide for their individual likes and dislikes, the results may be less than satisfactory. When students take the competency test, they may not show hoped-for gains in proficiency, no matter how carefully and thoroughly teachers have instructed them. Staff frustration mounts as parents and the public complain of the school's inability to deliver a program that works. An unexpected and uncomfortable situation arises because of an aspect of materials selection that was never considered.

The Concept of Congruency

To understand the relationship between the instructional materials selected for a basic skills program and the results the program can achieve, it's necessary to isolate the two major parts of any skills-based program— the *activities* that take place during instruction and the *assessment procedures* that are used to measure the results of that instruction. In today's evidence-oriented educational atmosphere, assessment procedures have taken on new importance. Basic skills programs, more often than not, are associated with some sort of formal testing program, which is almost always designed by a group other than those who create the basic skills instructional materials. Test publishers, for example, rarely create instructional materials to match their examinations. Although materials may be accompanied by sets of progress-monitoring examinations, those tests are seldom accepted as *the* competency exam.

Up to now, testing specialists and teaching specialists have each been concerned only with their own areas. Test developers have been thinking measurement while instructional materials developers have been thinking instruction. Neither group has been concerned about the match between their work. Fortunately, there is one important similarity between them that may compensate for their separate approaches: each group follows the same development process in creating its product. Both begin by isolating their *targets*. For the test developers, these targets are the basic skills to be measured. Their task is to define those skills clearly enough so that test questions can be written assessing the learner's mastery of the skills. Test developers must determine the precise *nature of the skill* as well as the *content* and the *performance mode* to be used to measure attainment of that skill.

In designing a mathematics test, a test developer might select problem solving as one skill to be measured. The developer must determine the nature of this skill. Will it be conceptualized as, for example, the ability to arrive at an accurate solution to a problem when given the exact numerical data necessary to compute that solution? Or will it be defined more broadly as, for instance, the ability to generate alternative solution strategies for use in a problem setting? Quite clearly, the first conceptualization of problem solving will yield test questions that are quite different from those generated by the second definition of the skill.

After the nature of the skill has been defined, the content to be used in measuring learner proficiency must be selected. Will students be solving problems that are abstract and purely theoretical, or will the problems be drawn from real-life situations and experiences? The content selected will determine the nature and the difficulty of the test questions.

Finally, the performance mode for testing must be stipulated. Will students be given a problem and a choice of several answers, or will they be required to work out their own answers? What criteria will be used to evaluate the correctness and incorrectness of responses?

By the time a test developer has determined the nature of a skill and the nature of the content and performance mode to be used in measuring that skill, a very definite testing target has been established.

A well-defined testing target

Developers of instructional materials also must establish targets for their work. Writers creating a set of basic skills mathematics materials might decide to use problem solving as one unit in a set of materials. When the materials are used, the instruction students receive and the activities they are asked to complete will depend on the writers' conceptualization of the skill, the content chosen to illustrate explanations and problems, and the performance modes selected for student activities. These developers also have established clear-cut targets.

A well-defined teaching target

Because tests and materials each are based on targets, the degree of *congruency* between a given set of materials and a given test can be determined by comparing the targets associated with each. Such a comparison should result in one of the following three states. It may be discovered that the targets are totally incongruent.

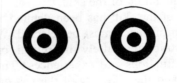

Totally incongruent targets

There may be some degree of overlap.

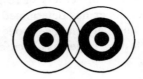

Targets that are somewhat the same

When instructional materials and assessment procedures are *entirely congruent,* the two targets become one and the same.

Totally congruent targets

The Importance of Congruency

Determining how well targets for instructional materials and basic skills tests match is extremely important. It also can be quite difficult. The task requires analyzing each component separately to devise as clear a picture as possible of the nature of each target. Often there are no detailed descriptive schemes accompanying either a test or a set of instructional materials. The potential matchmaker must attempt to devise these descriptions after the fact. Other times, the description that is provided may be more misleading than true. The same label may be applied to two quite different skills. Two different sets of mathematics materials, for example, might contain units on "problem solving," which bear little real resemblance to each other. The individuals responsible for congruency-analysis must be attentive enough to detect such disparities. They must never assume that the name given to a skill defines that skill. There are probably as many different versions of any single basic skill as there are materials and tests to match it.

Although it isn't easy to determine the congruency between various sets of materials and a program's test targets, the comparison must be made if positive instructional results are to occur. When a school's staff understands the relationship between the two sets of targets, they will certainly realize what is at stake for them.

Time on task and *appropriate practice* are two of the most powerful research-derived insights about the effects of instruction. These principles tell us that teachers must instruct students and then give them ample opportunities to practice the instructed skills. Each time students use a set of instructional materials, they practice the skills promoted by those materials. Their task-oriented time is being devoted to the particular targets associated with the materials. If the materials' targets are congruent with the tests' targets, then the more student time that is spent using the materials, the more dramatic the improvement in test results should be. If, however, the materials' targets do not match the tests' targets, then the test results will not necessarily measure the classroom instruction.

Teachers may do a first-rate instructional job using outstanding instructional materials. Nevertheless, *whenever instructors and materials are promoting targets other than the ones that will be assessed, the results will be disappointing.* Unless test targets can be changed to coincide with instructional targets (a highly unlikely possibility if the tests are mandated rather than optional), instructional efforts to improve student performance on those tests will continually fail. It will not be the quality of teaching skills or the degree of teacher dedication that is at fault. Teachers simply will have been aiming at the wrong targets.

An Example of Target-Matching

The following illustration offers a possible solution to the problem of mismatched instructional and measurement targets. It also demonstrates how a principal and a school's staff might go about applying the concept of congruency when selecting basic skills instructional materials.

The example itself, although hypothetical, is based on materials that are part of the Detroit High School Proficiency Program—a minimum competency assessment program used in the Detroit, Michigan, public schools. This program has as its measurement targets 12 basic skills, four each in reading, writing, and mathematics. Specially designed instructional materials that are entirely congruent with those targets have been devised and distributed throughout the district. Local schools also have the option of selecting instructional materials on their own.

One of the four reading skills is titled "Identifying Main Ideas." The description of that skill, provided in a program manual supplied to each teacher in the high schools, is as follows:

After reading a selection from a news story, a magazine, or a general information publication, the student is to identify its main idea by choosing from four statements the one which most accurately and comprehensively presents the central point of that selection.

One school's staff decided that it wanted to purchase basic skills reading materials that could be used in promoting the main idea skill. A preliminary survey turned up the following three options.

1. A reading series that contains a unit entitled "Reading for the Main Idea." The reading selections in this unit range from short stories to poems and plays. Students are to respond to these selections by composing an appropriate title for each one and by comparing their title with the author's title for the selection.

2. A vocabulary-building program that includes a group of exercises on "Developing the Main Idea." Each exercise requires the student to read a short article and choose the correct word to fill each of a number of blanks in that selection. Each blank represents a word deleted from the text. Students are to use context clues as well as their sense for the overall meaning of the passage in supplying the missing words.

3. A language-arts workbook that offers a section on "Finding the Main Idea." This section presents real-life content such as business letters, reports, editorials, and first person essays. Writing directly in the workbook, students are to underline the main idea sentence in each paragraph of a selection. If they cannot find a single sentence containing the main idea, they are to write a topic sentence that they feel would be appropriate.

The evaluation committee members found all materials well-written, instructionally sound, and particularly appealing to high school students—especially to the more reluctant learners. What the reviewers were keen enough to realize, however, was that not one of the three options would serve their needs. None of the materials contained a skill that matched the main idea skill in their testing program. That program requires students to compose a single-sentence statement that accurately and comprehensively presents the central point of a reading selection. Neither titling a selection (Option 1), nor supplying some of its words (Option 2), nor even finding its topic sentences (Option 3) is an *equivalent* reading skill. They may be related skills, and they may seem to "mix and match" well, but in reality they represent three entirely different competencies. Furthermore, the content of the materials does not coincide with the reading selections presented in the test. Quite wisely, the committee members rejected all three options and decided to keep looking for more suitable materials.

Some Potential Pitfalls

Congenial colleagues, sparkling superficialities, and *relaxed rigor* represent three major obstacles to effective match-making. Forewarned of these problems, a principal may be able to avoid them.

The first obstacle—congenial colleagues—reflects a problem caused by staff members who are good natured and don't want to offend. Even though they may not agree with the judgments of others on the faculty, they demur rather than dissent. As a result, even if they recognize that proposed materials will not match, they are reluctant to share their concerns. Their analysis never gets heard and hence goes unheeded. Principals who are aware of this "nice person" phenomenon may wish to seek out the more outspoken and assertive of their teachers to serve as leaders in materials selection groups.

Sparkling superficialities are brought to each school through the courtesy of American enterprise and the entrepreneurial spirit. The educational publishing industry realizes that back-to-basics readily translates into big bucks if instructional materials are shrewdly packaged and marketed. Hence, basic skills banners now adorn almost every materials catalog in the country, and magic buzz words such as "real-life skills" and "functional tasks" are used to promote almost every basic skills product. Slick packaging and clever merchandising are hard to resist, but principals and teachers must become effective consumers who are alert to a product's true worth rather than just its packaging.

Of the three obstacles, relaxed rigor may be the hardest to overcome. It is difficult, demanding work to analyze instructional materials and assessment targets in enough detail to determine if they are congruent. It is much easier to relax one's standards and let potential mismatches slip by. It does not take much effort to apply loose standards since almost any targets will be judged congruent if the matching criteria are general enough. The easy path is rarely the best one, and the stakes are too high to permit such leniency. Administrators must remain alert to ensure that quality control mechanisms are built into every materials review operation.

Five Key Steps

The following five steps summarize the actions a principal or supervisor might take in implementing basic skills instructional materials selection.

1. Select teachers for curriculum and materials selection committees who can think clearly and analytically and who are able to assert themselves professionally.

2. Provide selection committees with clear definitions of the basic skills targets that are to be tested.

3. Require committees to generate clear definitions of the basic skills target in any instructional materials considered for development or adoption.

4. Insist that committees justify their learning materials selections on the basis of congruence with the program's target skills.

5. Monitor the committees' work to ensure that rigorous quality control standards are applied.

Making a Match

It takes hard work, a committed faculty, and perceptive administrators to develop basic skills instructional programs perfectly matched to appropriate targets. Frequently, commercial materials that are congruent to local targets cannot be found and must be developed locally. The school's leaders can offer support to such development efforts, and successful materials can be shared among schools facing the same basic skills targets. At first it may be difficult to convince teachers that their willingness to mix and match a wide range of easily available materials really works to their disadvantage. Once they can be shown the benefits of aiming at the right targets, they should become confirmed believers. Increased student achievement should help make those beliefs last.

References

Baker, Robert L., and Schultz, Richard E., eds. *Instructional Product Development*. New York: Van Nostrand Reinhold Company, 1971.

Popham, W. James, and Lindheim, Elaine. *Making Minimum Competency Programs Work*. Los Angeles: Instructional Objectives Exchange, 1979.

Tyler, Louise L.; Klein, M. Frances; and others. *Evaluating and Choosing Curriculum and Instructional Materials*. Los Angeles: Educational Resource Associates, Inc., 1976.

9.

Basic Skills
and Measurement Basics

W. James Popham

American education, as never before, is becoming evidence-oriented. Citizens are clamoring for higher levels of demonstrated pupil achievement. Legislators are demanding that students display minimal competencies before they receive high school diplomas. School boards are pressuring teachers for evidence of their educational effectiveness. Superintendents are entreating principals to stimulate higher levels of pupil performance. In American schooling, rhetoric about high quality will no longer suffice. Everyone, it seems, wants results!

In an evidence-oriented enterprise, those who control the evidence-producing mechanisms, in reality, control the entire enterprise. In education, we produce evidence of quality chiefly through the use of tests. While there are other legitimate indicators of education effectiveness, many American educators have fostered the perception that the quality of our public school system is adequately reflected by pupil scores on standardized achievement tests. This was particularly true during the 30s, 40s, and 50s, when students were scoring rather well on achievement tests. It isn't surprising, then, that the public still considers student test performance as the gauge of the quality of education.

Since student test performance plays such a prominent role in the public's perception of education quality, it is clear that secondary school administrators must become familiar with the most prominent applications, both proper and improper, of educational tests. This need for greater familiarity with current thinking regarding educational tests meshes most meaningfully with today's emphasis on the promotion of basic skills. Secondary schools are now under increasing pressure to advance students' basic skills and to produce evidence in the form of test scores that basic skills have actually been achieved.

105

Relating Tests Scores to School Procedures

While it may be true that national concerns about basic skills abound, do these concerns really affect what goes on in schools?

Yes, in several ways, depending on the types of basic skills tests the school uses and the inferences that are drawn from students' performance on those tests. In particular, schools use basic skills test results in making decisions about student promotion, student remediation, and the quality of instruction taking place in the school.

Student Promotion

Most of the minimum competency testing programs in approximately 40 states focus on basic skills. In many of these programs, a youngster must pass a competency test at or above a specific level of proficiency prior to graduation. Both Florida and California have statewide test-based graduation systems. Although not all secondary schools currently face the prospect of test-based promotions, such a possibility clearly exists.

Student Remediation

In many settings where grade level advancement or high school diplomas are not based on students' basic skills test scores, those scores do play a role in identifying students who need remedial assistance of one sort or another. Indeed, numerous states, including South Carolina and Texas, now have legislatively mandated programs of remedial instruction for students who fail to reach specified levels of competence in basic skills.

Quality Determination

In an increasing number of major school districts, average pupil test scores are reported annually on a school-by-school basis. The leadership of the Washington, D.C., public schools makes no bones about the reason it introduced such school-by-school reporting. It was, in the words of former D.C. School Superintendent Vincent Reed, a scheme to make the district's principals and teachers more directly accountable to the public by openly displaying their relative success, or lack of success, in promoting pupil achievement.

Measurement Moxie

In a flagrant example of wishful thinking, educators widely believe that secondary school teachers are rather knowledgeable about testing.

After all, teachers dispense tests almost constantly and use the results to award grades.

Yet, when it comes to any genuine sophistication in measurement of knowledge, most secondary teachers are utterly handicapped. The distressing truth is that precious few of them know very much at all about testing—other than what they recall from their own experiences as students when they were on the receiving end of tests. If you ask most secondary teachers to distinguish between such fundamental measurement concepts as *validity* and *reliability,* they'd probably be forced to focus on disparities in spelling. If they do know the rudiments of measurement—perhaps gleaned from teacher education courses in the care and feeding of multiple-choice test items—those notions will usually be associated with traditional conceptions of educational testing, conceptions that are largely inappropriate for today's basic skills testing requirements.

Norm- and Criterion-Referenced Tests

In the early 60s, American educators found the expressions "norm-referenced test" and "criterion-referenced test" added to our educational lexicon. Although there wasn't much dispute about the meaning of the phrase norm-referenced test, since those were the tests we'd been using for decades, it took several years before a consensus definition emerged for criterion-referenced tests. The distinction between these two measurement strategies is pivotal in the assessment of basic skills.

A *norm-referenced* test establishes the status of an examinee in relation to the performance of other examinees who have completed the same test. The examinee's performance is, therefore, *referenced* to that of a norm group. Norm-referenced tests can focus on aptitude (such as one's academic potential) or achievement (such as one's reading skills). In basic skills assessment, we are concerned chiefly with norm-referenced achievement tests. Student scores on norm-referenced tests are customarily converted to percentiles or some similar vehicle that conveys a relative interpretation to the norm group's performance.

A *criterion-referenced test* establishes the status of an examinee with respect to a well-defined class of behaviors, such as a clearly described skill in mathematics. While a norm-referenced test provides its chief meaning by comparing a student's score to that of other students, a criterion-referenced test attempts to isolate how well the student can master a specified skill or attribute. A criterion-referenced test focuses on the *clarity of description* associated with the skill or attribute being measured. To illustrate, with a well-defined criterion-referenced test we might determine that a student "had mastered 75 percent of the test items used to assess mastery of the skill being measured." In this sense, a norm-referenced measure provides *relative* interpretations while a criterion-referenced test provides *absolute* interpretations.

It is often impossible to distinguish between a norm-referenced test and a criterion-referenced test merely by looking at the test items. Indeed, one might encounter a number of identical items on norm- and criterion-referenced tests. To distinguish between these two testing strategies, one needs to consult the discriptive information on the test's measured skills. One also needs to know a good deal about how the test was originally constructed.

Since norm-referenced tests have been with us for decades, they are a generally well-known commodity and our standards for judging them are refined. As a consequence, a number of excellent norm-referenced testing instruments are available.

To the contrary, and chiefly because we've only been working seriously on criterion-referenced tests for a dozen or so years, the technical base of criterion-referenced testing is far more primitive. Thus, the quality of existing criterion-referenced tests varies dramatically. There are relatively small numbers of well constructed criterion-referenced tests at our disposal. Indeed, because most available criterion-referenced tests have been produced expediently rather than rigorously, they should be sent scurrying to the paper-shredder.

Sophistication in judging criterion-referenced tests becomes particularly crucial since, for the most part, *norm-referenced achievement tests can play no meaningful role in satisfying today's basic skill assessment needs.* This is not to say there is no educational role for norm-referenced tests. There are numerous situations in which a student's performance on a norm-referenced test can prove most useful. Typically, such situations arise in fixed quota settings where there are more applications than openings for a given program. However, for the sorts of basic skills measurement problems faced by today's secondary schools, norm-referenced tests are of only limited use.

Shortcomings of Norm-Referenced Achievement Tests

It is not sufficient merely to assert that "norm-referenced tests are unsuitable." A solid and convincing rationale must be supplied for abandoning the very tests that educators have touted for so many years.

Imprecise Descriptions

The first problem with using norm-referenced achievement tests in basic skills assessment programs is that the nature of what's being measured by the tests is inadequately described. This shortcoming stems from the general survey nature of many norm-referenced achievement tests. They are supposed to yield a relative (in reference to the norm group) estimate of a student's knowledge of, for example, "mathematics fundamentals." Broad survey instruments do not need to be well described since it is usually sufficient for a survey to provide only a general notion of what is being measured. Since there are such substantial curricular variations in different parts of the nation, it is also true that commercial test publishers are reluctant to spell out precisely what their tests measure. The more precisely the tests's emphases are described, the less likely that those emphases will match a local district's curriculum. Commercial test publishers, therefore, provide exceedingly vague descriptions of their wares. They hope to benefit from the Rorschach dividend—letting test purchasers see what they wish to see in the ink-blot descriptions of what's being measured.

Because of these diffuse descriptions, there are often *unrecognized mismatches* between what is tested and what is taught. Suppose, for example, that you are the principal of a high school in which the reading program emphasizes a set of highly applied "life-role" reading skills. However, the norm-referenced reading comprehension test chosen by your district's testing committee fails to tap these skills. Although your teachers are doing a dazzling job in promoting student mastery of life-role reading skills, your school's scores on the district test look like the teaching staff had been on summer vacation for 12 months.

Mismatches between what's tested and what's taught yield an erroneous picture of instructional effectiveness. Because descriptions of what's being measured are characteristically vague, it is almost impossible to match a school's (or district's) instructional emphases with what is being measured by a norm-referenced achievement test.

A related problem arising from fuzzy descriptions of measured behavior is that most norm-referenced achievement tests provide no clear targets for instruction. It is impossible for teachers to design an instructional sequence that is genuinely germane to a set of intended outcomes if those outcomes are not thoroughly understood. Generalized descriptions associated with norm-referenced tests preclude the creation of truly on-target teaching.

Nothing is more frustrating to teachers than to have administrators deliver pep messages such as "Boost our students' scores on the district's norm-referenced achievement test!" Without a lucid understanding of what that test's measured skills actually are, the teachers are aiming at fog.

Psychometric Monkey-Business

The second major deficit in norm-referenced achievement tests is more technical. Throughout the years, a series of clever technical procedures has been developed for norm-referenced tests by psychometrists (a ritzy name for testers). The problem is that some of these procedures result in the creation of achievement tests that are fundamentally insensitive to instruction. Tests that are insensitive to instruction, of course, fail to reflect accurately the true effectiveness of teaching. Even the efforts of a cracker-jack collection of teachers will appear to be ineffectual if student perform-ance on norm-referenced achievement tests fail to improve over time.

How can psychometric procedures traditionally employed with norm-referenced tests cripple the capabilities of such tests to detect effects of fine instruction? Remember, in order for a norm-referenced test to do its job properly, student scores on the test must be quite varied. The more varia-bility in scores, the better; since to make fine-grained percentile compari-sons among students, it is clearly necessary that those students attain different scores. If, on a 100-item norm-referenced achievement test, almost all students answered either 71 or 72 items correctly, there would be little chance to make sensible comparisons among students. Norm-referenced test developers, therefore, strive to spread examinee scores over as large a range of points as possible.

Another advantage of highly varied test scores is that such variability markedly increases the reliability coefficient of the test. Other factors being equal, tests with higher reliability coefficients are more marketable than tests with lower reliability coefficients. Thus, to permit more sensitive comparisons among examinees and to heighten a test's reliability, devel-opers of norm-referenced tests try diligently to produce varied scores among examinees.

Now, however, this psychometric plot thickens. A test item that does the best job in spreading out examinee scores is one that is answered correctly by only 50 percent of the examinees. If it is answered correctly by a substantially larger proportion of the examinees, say 80 percent or higher, then that item will be removed from the test when it is revised. Indeed, even in the original development of a set of norm-referenced test items, item-writers will try to shy away from items on which too many examinees might perform well. Items that don't do their share in spreading out examinees' total test peformance have no place in a norm-referenced test.

Now comes the clincher. Test items on which students perform well are frequently those that cover topics teachers thought important enough to stress. The better teachers are, the more they emphasize important topics, the better their students will perform on items covering those topics. But the better their students perform on those items, the less likely that those items will remain on the test. *A norm-referenced achievement test, particularly one that has been revised often, tends to exclude the very items that cover the most important things teachers teach.*

To produce varied examinee responses to norm-referenced test items, the test constructors often create items that, in order for students to answer correctly, require familiarity with subtle verbal nuances. These technical procedures result in achievement tests that measure, in addition to what the student learns in school, *the nature of the student's prior verbal experience.* If that verbal experience coincides with the verbal nuances in the test items, then the student is in good shape. If the student's verbal experience is not consonant with the semantic subtleties in the test items, then teachers will find it nearly impossible to help the student achieve high test scores.

Psychometric procedures associated with the creation and refinement of norm-referenced achievement tests tend to render them largely insensitive in detecting the consequences of effective instruction. Thus, the quality of a top-flight instructional program is often not truly reflected in students' scores on norm-referenced achievement tests. Often such test scores are influenced by what students bring to school rather than by what they learn at school. Conversely, because of their instructional insensitivity, norm-referenced tests tend to mask a truly poor instructional program.

In review, then, imprecise descriptiveness and inherent tendencies toward instructional insensitivity render norm-referenced achievement tests largely unsuitable for assessing student mastery of basic skills. As indicated earlier, norm-referenced tests do have a number of other important applications, but those do not include evaluating or designing a basic skills instructional program. To be sure, using a norm-referenced achievement test is preferable to using no tests at all. But there is a preferable alternative—using criterion-referenced tests. Let's briefly consider that measurement alternative in relationship to the assessment of secondary basic skills.

A Winning Criterion-Referenced Test

Evaluative Factor No. 1: Descriptive Clarity

A well-constructed criterion-referenced test will contain unambiguous descriptions of each skill measured by the test. These descriptions should be so precise that if different teachers were asked to independently create test items from the skill descriptions, the resulting items would be remarkably similar.

In general, an instructional objective does *not* constitute a sufficiently clear description for a set of criterion-referenced test items. Instructional objectives, even if stated behaviorally, are too large to delimit satisfactorily the nature of the items measuring a given skill. Objectives must be accompanied by additional descriptive materials to meaningfully define what the test items measure. These accompanying descriptive materials are frequently called test specifications.

Evaluative Factor No. 2: A Manageable Number of Skills

American educators learned an important lesson in the late '60s and early '70s when behavioral objectives were billed as the ultimate answer to a teacher's pedagogical yearnings. We learned that long lists of hyperspecific and miniscule objectives had little, if any, impact on a teacher's instructional decisions. Too many targets turned out to be no target at all. Some school district officials still labor under the delusion that the smaller the segment of learner behavior objectives embody, the more useful the objectives are to teachers. This is folly.

Faced with a nearly endless list of small-scope objectives, most sensible teachers simply disregard them. Teachers are, quite properly, overwhelmed by all that specificity. If, as in some districts, teachers are formally obliged to record each student's status on oodles of objectives, then we had best prepare ourselves to provide psychiatric assistance to scores of teachers who will soon suffer from recordkeeping-induced psychoses.

Criterion-referenced tests that focus on a small number of more significant skills—skills that subsume a number of lesser, en route skills—are preferable. For example, the high school proficiency examination used by the Detroit Public Schools measures only four skills in reading, four skills in mathematics, and four skills in writing. All 12 of these basic skills, however, are significant skills that coalesce many lower-order skills. Similarly, South Carolina now has statewide basic skills tests that measure only six reading skills, five mathematics skills, and five writing skills.

Teachers will heed a small number of well-defined skills, particularly if those skills are accurately measured by well-constructed criterion-referenced tests. In choosing how many skills a criterion-referenced test should measure, we have a classic case where, as usual, less is more.

Evaluative Factor No. 3: Enough Items Per Skill

To reliably assess student mastery of a particular skill, the criterion-referenced test must contain a sufficient number of items per skill. Two or three items per skill are not sufficient. In Detroit, for example, where the type of high school diploma hinges on the results of students' proficiency test scores, 10 items per skill are used. In South Carolina, where test results are used only to identify students who need remedial assistance, six items per skill are used in the statewide tests. Clearly, the use of test results should determine how many items per skill are necessary. Rarely, however, will only two or three items suffice.

Evaluative Factor No. 4: Instructional Implications

Quite recently, it has been recognized that criterion-referenced tests can be constructed to assist the teacher's instructional design decisions. If test developers are attentive to the instructional implications of rules devised for creating the test's items, familiarity with those rules can benefit instructional planning.

Ideally, the criterion-referenced test will have instructional guidelines that set forth, in language teachers can understand, the instructionally relevant dimensions of the test items measuring each skill assessed in the test. If a test's designers were cognizant of the potential instructability for skills *measured in that test,* teachers conversant with the nature of the tested skills could design and implement more effective instruction.

If constructed by instructionally alert developers, a criterion-referenced test can define a set of teachable skills so lucidly that *the test itself becomes a potent force for instructional improvement.* Instead of being an afterthought at the close of instruction, a properly conceptualized criterion-referenced test can trigger measurement-driven instructional improvement.

Teachers *and administrators* can become thoroughly conversant with the skills being measured. Students can practice exercises consonant with the targeted skills, thus providing the *time-on-task* so necessary to effective learning. Clear descriptions of the target skills can be given to both students and parents.

Such a focused instructional enterprise is not "teaching-to-the-test" in the negative sense that one teaches toward a particular set of test items. To the contrary, this approach constitutes "teaching-to-the-skill," a highly effective and thoroughly legitimate instructional strategy.

Evaluative Factor No. 5: Comparability Indicators

One of the substantial virtues of norm-referenced tests is that they do provide us with normative data by which local educators and citizens can compare their students' test scores with those of other students across the nation. The public has a legitimate right to see how pupils' performances compare nationally. Thus, a criterion-referenced test should also provide a scheme by which its scores can be compared with a representative, national student sample.

If a criterion-referenced test does not contain a suitable set of normative data, then local district test personnel may want to create equivalency tables that link scores on the locally used criterion-referenced achievement tests. A number of defensible test-equating procedures available for this purpose have recently been described by measurement specialists. Indeed, since some federal funding requirements demand the use of nationally normed tests, or those that have been equated to nationally normed tests, it may be necessary to carry out such equating procedures if unnormed criterion-referenced tests are used.

In addition to these five important factors, there are other elements to consider in appraising a criterion-referenced test. The test's demonstrated reliability and validity, as well as its ease of administration and scoring, are also important. Nonetheless, these five evaluative factors can prove useful when distinguishing between criterion-referenced tests that are stellar and those that are stunted.

It should be noted that high-quality criterion-referenced tests are not easy to produce. Much rigorous intellectual attention is required to generate and refine a test's specifications and items. Ordinarily, production of such criterion-referenced tests is *not* an enterprise that local school districts can do successfully without substantial external assistance (for instance, from a state department of education or a private test-development agency). Teachers, although many of them are surely bright enough and verbally facile enough, are usually not interested in engaging in the meticulous work required to create a genuinely fine criterion-referenced testing instrument.

School district officials will ordinarily want to see if commercially available, "off-the-shelf," criterion-referenced tests suit their purposes. If none are available, then local test development should be undertaken with substantial external technical support.

Myriad Measures

The previous discussion is not exclusively about traditional paper-and-pencil tests. One may conceptualize basic skills in such a way that they require the student to engage in some sort of observable performance. Performance measures are, in general, appraised in precisely the same fashion as discussed above. Well-fashioned performance measures, such as those that might tap learners' oral communication or artistic skills, can be as instrumental in improving a basic skills program as their more traditional paper-and-pencil counterparts. However, even more so than is true with customary paper-and-pencil tests, school systems will need considerable technical assistance if they are to develop criterion-referenced *performance* tests of high quality.

There has been no mention of *affective* assessment devices. We have been chiefly dealing with cognitive and psychomotor tests. Yet, one of the most critical assessment requirements associated with a basic skills instructional program deals with students' attitudes and interests rather than their cognitive skills.

As long as American educators use cognitive tests, make important decisions on the basis of their results, and supply only rhetoric in support of affective goals, it is predictable which sorts of emphases will be present in our schools. Affective dimensions, such as how students perceive themselves as learners, can be crucial in appraising the quality of a basic skills program. Principals should foster the use of affective assessment devices in connection with their district's or school's basic skills programs. A discussion of the ingredients of such measures, however, is beyond the scope of this analysis.

What's to Be Done?

Test results are playing an increasingly vital role in American education. Because of today's increased emphasis on basic skills instruction, those involved in fostering students' mastery of basic skills should become familiar with both the sensible as well as the senseless applications of educational tests. In this assessment analysis, norm-referenced achievement tests were judged to have limited utility in basic skills instructional programs. In contrast, criterion-referenced tests are potentially powerful tools in designing and evaluating basic skills programs.

What are the implications of this analysis for the typically harassed secondary school administrator? Assuming the foregoing observations are accurate, what's to be done about it?

Well, there would seem to be two readily identifiable steps that might be taken. The first step is to enhance staff sophistication regarding assessment issues in basic skills programs. A principal might present a summary of these comments or, perhaps, reproduce copies of this analysis for each staff member. In any event, a thorough discussion of major testing issues by the school's instructional staff would seem essential.

More aggressively, a principal might provide teachers with a minicourse on modern measurement, perhaps five or six hours in duration, taught by a measurement specialist who is up to date on advances in criterion-referenced testing. Some so-called measurement experts are still so enamoured of traditional norm-referenced testing that they dare not embrace current advances in assessment. Such Neanderthals must be avoided.

There are several *recent* textbooks designed for tests and measurement courses that might be provided as resources for the teaching staff. Be sure that the text being considered gives ample attention to criterion-referenced measurement. Although I have recently written just such a sterling volume, modesty prevents me (almost) from mentioning it.

Perhaps one or two teachers can be persuaded to become the school's resident expert(s) on testing. They could take an extension course on modern measurement advances, carry out some independent reading, and share their insights with the rest of the staff during inservice colloquies.

As I have stressed repeatedly throughout this chapter, the impact of testing has increased exponentially in recent years. Secondary school officials must recognize that testing has become far too important to leave to the testers.

10.

Leadership for Effective School Procedures

Asa G. Hilliard

For several decades, Americans have expressed concern over the failure of large numbers of students to achieve basic skills. We have asked why Johnny can't read, add, and write. This concern has been voiced at all levels of the educational system, from elementary schools through the university. University professors and officials complain bitterly that they are required to provide a disproportionate amount of resources for student remediation in reading, writing, and computation. Little consensus exists about the origin of the problem or the means to solve it. At every level of education, the blame for Johnny's poor achievement is aimed at the educators who taught Johnny before.

Numerous studies have been reported in the professional literature and in the popular news media that document the achievement decline in basic school skills. Perhaps the most revealing barometer of this decline has been Scholastic Aptitude Test scores. While there have been some debates regarding the content validity of the SAT and other similar measures, no one has argued that failing students have actually mastered the skills purportedly measured by such tests. Indeed, valid standardized tests or not, we would be hard pressed to discover evidence of general school success in teaching basic skills to the masses of our students at any level.

Immediately, the question arises: Is the present level of student achievement the highest we can expect? *Can* student achievement be improved? There are those who argue that the nation has already reached maximum performance potential in basic skills. In fact, some educators believe that equal educational opportunities for all children—which have ensured that many learners who were regarded as uneducable or of limited educational potential in the past are now part of the general school population—account for the overall decline in SAT scores. And other, more

117

cynical, theories persist. Nevertheless, even educators who disagree about the root causes of the problem at least tacitly agree that its magnitude precludes any likelihood that significant improvements and changes can be made quickly. It is precisely this forecast that must be examined. Our major question, then, must be: Can educational leadership reverse negative outcomes for students in the basic skills?

Some Explanations for Low Student Achievement

Abundant data have been accumulated to support the argument that children fail in school primarily for reasons that have little to do with what happens in schools.[1] In some cases, such conclusions result from an improper interpretation of studies on school populations. In other cases, the conclusions may be a direct expression of researchers' assumptions. Some explanations suggest that certain children are deprived of "culture" and consequently are unable to profit from school experiences for which "culture" is a prerequisite.[2] Other researchers have concluded that failing learners are intellectually deficient.[3] Still others have argued that a learner's low socioeconomic level explains a low school achievement level.

Obviously, "culture," "intellect," and "socioeconomic status" are factors that may not be amenable to short-term intervention. These are regarded as global, pervasive, stable, contextual, or genetic factors—factors that determine the "equipment," material, and experiences the student brings to learning. These factors may also contribute to ceilings or floors on the motivational levels found among learners. Regardless of which explanation is favored or how any given explanation is theorized, the result among educators is to adopt the view that schools can do little, if anything, to change student outcomes since the things that need changing lie outside the scope of educators' responsibility.

The stability of the correlation among intelligence test scores, school achievement test scores, and some school grades appears to support the view that schools are powerless to change learner outcomes. Similarly, certain studies of differential experiences or offerings among schools appear to show that school experiences do not contribute to a change in outcomes for learners. In the Coleman study, for example, the variation in

---

[1] J. S. Coleman and others, *Equality of Educational Opportunity* (Washington, D.C.: U.S. Government Printing Office, 1966).

[2] H. Ginsberg, *The Myth of the Deprived Child: Poor Children's Intellect and Education* (Englewood Cliffs, N.J.: Prentice-Hall, 1972).

[3] A. Jensen, *Bias in Mental Testing* (New York: Free Press, 1980).

physical facilities among different school sites appears to make little difference in terms of learner outcome.[4]

Further, fairly straightforward scientific methodologies are available to describe distinctions among cultural groups. It can also be shown that these cultural distinctions are associated with socioeconomic status. The most frequent interpretation of this association asserts that the combination of certain cultural variations and associated low socioeconomic status *cause* poor school performance among learners. These combined factors produce a student whose normal intellectual faculties, if indeed they are normal, atrophy as a consequence of the student's environment and no longer serve as effective and efficient resources for learning.

Were these data and interpretations the only ones available to educators, there might be little reason to question the conclusions that stem from them or to become unduly concerned about widespread evidence of poor performance among large segments of our population. However, such is not the case. There are other data that provide an entirely different picture.

The Positive Effects of Schools

Over the years, many educators around the nation have actually demonstrated the results of quality school experiences on basic skills achievement in a variety of school settings. However, these educators' experiences and school operations have seldom been documented formally. Formal observations would have revealed that many low-performing schools have been "turned around" by a good educational leader. It is also evident that these same schools, serving essentially the same types of students, can just as quickly return to low performance levels upon the departure of that educational leader. There are many secondary schools located in neighborhoods or in cities where low achievement is the traditional expectation, yet high performance for graduates has been demonstrated and, in some instances, over long periods of time.[5] In a few cases, researchers, operating on limited resources, have identified such schools.

However, the mainstream of educational interest and activity among researchers and policy makers seems to have concentrated on analyzing schools that have failed or are simply nondescript, on bemoaning the fact of ordinary and lackluster school achievement, and on applying these

---

[4] Coleman and others, 1966.

[5] R. Edmonds, "Some Schools Work and More Can," *Social Policy* (March/April 1979): 29-32.

results to education, generally. It is not at all clear why so many educators have overlooked startling examples of high student achievement in schools where such achievement would not ordinarily be expected. When documentation was limited or nonexistent, it was easy to point to such schools as merely "exceptions to the rule." They were seen as accidents or as flukes. In fact, the measurement criteria for achievement or even the reporter's honesty about these exceptional schools might be questioned. The general pattern of research grouped poorly functioning classrooms in poorly functioning schools together with excellent classrooms and excellent schools. By aggregating the results from classrooms and schools and by taking the average of such aggregates, the actual significant effects of special instruction or of special schools is obscured.

Within the past few decades, however, educational research methodology and interest have caught up with the realities of secondary school performance.[6] New questions have been asked, new methodologies have been employed, and higher levels of resources have been put at the disposal of researchers. The results have been quite interesting, especially if selected findings are combined. *These findings are solid, replicable, and valid,* even though they may be selected from among a variety of findings which, for the most part, are not relevant to our concerns. To select appropriate findings we must ask if there is anything special about successful schools and what criteria are used in designating a school as successful.

In the Beginning Teacher Evaluation Study (BTES)—which was initiated at the request of the California Teacher Preparation and Licensing Commission, and conducted first by the Educational Testing Service and later by the Far West Regional Laboratory for Educational Research and Development—"successful" schools were compared to "unsuccessful" schools. Standardized achievement test scores of children in the schools were the criterion for determining whether a school was successful or not. When systematic observations of teaching processes were made in the successful and unsuccessful schools, an empirical base for fundamental insights was established. A compelling new refinement from the BTES Study was added to the general way in which many educators view classrooms. Specifically, it was shown that children succeeded in classrooms where teachers were able to organize instruction and to supervise it in such a way that most students spent the major part of their time in class on the

---

[6] D. Berliner, W. Tikunoff, and B. Ward, *Beginning Teacher Evaluation Study* (San Francisco: Far West Laboratory for Educational Research and Development, 1976); R. Edmonds, 1979; J. A. Stallings, *Follow-Through Program Classroom Observation Evaluation,* 1971-72 (Menlo Park, Calif.: Stanford Research Institute, 1973).

task of learning the subject matter that was supposed to be taught. Consequently, "time on task" emerged in educational circles as a major variable, even a goal, of successful instruction. Other researchers, such as Jere Brophy and Jane Stallings, have also been successful in showing that classrooms where children succeed are quite different in terms of instruction from classrooms where children fail. In these examples, the level or unit of analysis was most frequently the classroom. It was left to Ron Edmonds an his associates to use the school as the unit of analysis.

To answer the question, "Do any schools work?" Edmonds and associates *disaggregated the data* so that the performance of individual schools could be identified. Then, looking at nationwide samples of successful and unsuccessful schools, they were able to discover schools located in the most unlikely areas in which students were attaining high achievement levels in the basic skills. Another important step remained, however. Edmonds and his associates took that additional step by analyzing the effective schools in contrast to ineffective schools. They performed systematic, fine-grained observations of schools to determine distinguishing factors in the two sets of schools. The following factors and principles summarize Edmond's findings:

1. Staffs of schools that work heavily emphasize basic reading and mathematics.

2. Staffs of schools that work believe that *all students can master the basic school objectives*. They also believe their principals share these objectives.

3. Staffs of schools that work expect higher educational achievement from students than staffs in schools that do not work.

4. Teachers and principals in schools that work assume responsibility for student achievement in reading and mathematics.

5. More time is spent on basic skills in schools that work than in schools that do not work.

6. The principal acts as an instructional leader, is assertive, is a disciplinarian, and assumes responsibility for the evaluation of basic skills achievement in schools that work.

7. Educational accountability is accepted by staffs of schools that work.

8. Teachers are less satisfied with their children's progress and with existing conditions in schools that work.

9. In schools that work, there is less parental involvement in improving the schools.

10. There is less emphasis on paraprofessional staff, compensatory education placement, and programmed instruction; fewer staff members are involved in reading instruction in schools that work than in schools that do not work.

The Beginning Teacher Evaluation Study and the studies of effective schools by Ron Edmonds and others are in no way isolated examples of the power of schools and teaching practices to change learning achievement levels for most students. Many educators are able to show dramatic, consistent, replicable, successful results with learners who ordinarily are expected to be very low performers. Feuerstein has demonstrated that the teaching of cognitive skills can actually result in the modification of cognitive structures.[7] Fuller has shown through her work with retarded students that those who are taught to read often spontaneously teach themselves to write as a by-product of that learning experience![8] William Johntz, National Director of the 15-year-old Project SEED, has developed a methodology for teaching children abstract, conceptually oriented college level mathematics, which has been taught to many teachers.[9] Johntz and his trained teachers have been able to show dramatic gains, both in arithmetic and in mathematics objectives, by children in kindergarten through sixth grade. Paulo Freire in Brazil and Lotte and Allen Marcus in California, directors of the literacy program, English on Wheels, have obtained rapid, dramatic, and consistent results when teaching literacy skills to low-performing, migrant farm-worker adult populations.[10]

One may ask, in the face of such startling results, how it is possible for researchers to continue finding that school practices appear to make little difference with large numbers of low-performing children. The answer to this question appears to be quite simple. *In almost every instance, such research is conducted without systematic attention to the nature of the actual instruction offered to children.*

When instruction is not comparable, the achievement results for learners cannot be compared in any meaningful way. Almost any casual observer can note the vast differences in quality of educational offerings among schools in low socioeconomic areas—not only in terms of differen-

---

[7] Reuven Feuerstein, *The Dynamic Assessment of Retarded Performers* (Baltimore: University Park Press, 1979); and *Instrumental Enrichment* (Baltimore: University Park Press, 1980).

[8] Renee Fuller, *In Search of the IQ Correlation* (Stonybrook, N.Y.: Ball-Stick-Bird Publishers, 1977).

[9] For information on Project SEED, write to Project SEED, 2336-A McKinley Avenue, Berkeley, California 94703.

[10] P. Freire, *Pedagogy of the Oppressed* (New York: Herder and Herder, 1968).

tial facilities, but also *in terms of differential teaching.* Empirical demonstrations of differences in the quality of instruction offered to excluded "minority" populations and to children occupying the lower rung of the socioeconomic ladder are easy to make. Yet traditional research on the effects of teaching or on the effects of schools has almost always been conducted without controlling the highly significant variable of *teaching quality.* Studies that show the success of learners is a function of schooling identify the precise nature of the educational intervention and measure the consistency of its application in the school setting.

School success does occur, in many cases, when certain specialized teaching interventions are offered. However, it would be a major error to conclude that low-performing students can be turned into high-performing students only if specialized teaching interventions are made. In fact, the main message of Edmonds' work is the extraordinary discovery that "ordinary, garden-variety schools" often achieve high levels of success with children. These schools are characterized primarily by systematic, sustained instruction, rather than by secret, unique, or magical methodologies. Therefore, we can say, based on empirical evidence, that a normal or even above-normal level of school achievement is well within the reach of almost all students. Schools can produce successful student achievement with regular teachers if appropriate pedagogical strategies are used and if appropriate school leadership is given. No special materials, equipment, or magic are required.

School Leadership and Basic Skills Achievement

The data we have looked at so far support the assertion that *teaching and school practices are primary factors responsible for basic school skills achievement among students.* By analyzing successful and unsuccessful schools, as measured by student achievement scores, we can discover the major effects of instruction on learners. This is not to say that school effects are the only effects. However, individual teachers and individual schools can be and have been responsible for *significant changes* in student achievement. The role of the principal in achieving positive change is primary. Every principal who wishes to ensure that a school's program is maximally effective can take certain explicit steps to do so. Among these steps are the following:

1. *Principals must be educational leaders.* As leaders, they must become familiar with as much of the research on successful schools as is humanly possible. The purpose of reviewing research is to develop confidence that school leaders and teachers together can produce desirable

conditions for student achievement. In addition, the research review may provide clues for program development and implementation.

2. *Principals must use every opportunity to become familiar with models of successful school operation.* There is no substitute for firsthand observation and participation, if possible, in successful school settings that are similar to a principal's assigned school.

3. *Principals must develop a repertoire of successful instructional strategies.* It is impossible for any single principal to be knowledgeable about all successful instructional strategies. However, principals' credibility with teachers and the confidence with which they can approach the leadership task depends in part on knowledge that success is possible and successful strategies are available.

An Important Conclusion: Students Are Capable

Far from being the educational goal, basic skills achievement really represents the minimum achievable standard for the vast majority of students served in our secondary schools. Our energy and resolve to attack the problem of basic skills learning should be increased by the fact that virtually all students who normally attend secondary schools in America are fully capable, with appropriate instruction, of mastering not only basic skills but also foreign languages, advanced abstract mathematics, and written and oral expression as well. It is unfortunate that so many professional educators have become resigned to the notion that large segments of pupils are doomed to failure. That at present many are doomed to failure, there can be no doubt. However, the reason for that unfortunate outcome has little to do with the learning limits of students. It has a great deal to do with what educators expect of students and especially with what those expectations lead educators to do for, and with, learners.

There is a body of research literature that focuses on the "expectancy effect" in education.[11] Numerous studies have shown that there is a strong association between the expectations that educators, especially teachers, hold of children and the eventual learning outcomes for those children. The results of expectancy research have been interpreted by some educators in a very narrow and perhaps erroneous way. Educators who accept the research say that teacher expectations *cause* student learning. That is to say, if a teacher expects low achievement, that becomes the cause for a student's low achievement. In fact, expectancy research shows that be-

---

[11] R. Rosenthal and L. Jacobson, *Pygmalion in the Classroom* (New York: Holt, Rinehart & Winston, 1968); R. E. Snow, *A Model Teacher Training System* (Stanford: Stanford Center for Research and Development in Teaching, 1972).

yond the association between educators' expectations and children's achievement is something much more fundamental. *Educator expectations change educator behavior toward children.* It is the *behavior* of educators, rather than the expectations per se, that affects children's outcomes. For example, teachers who have low expectations for children may fail to engage expected low performers for the same amount of instructional time as they do expected high performers. They may be less tolerant of answers given by low performers and may fail to follow up on questions to low performers. Therefore, the concern of educational leaders should be directed to teacher and administrator behavior, rather than expectations that are but symptoms.

If American educators looked beyond our boundaries to other nations, we would discover that it is possible for an entire nation to improve its educational system, including the basic skills. There are international examples of rapid literacy accomplishment as an outcome of a government's priority effort. The vast majority of our nation's students could be reading, writing, and counting at an acceptable level within less than 12 months if, as a nation, we established a high priority for these goals. Pending such a decision at the national level, individual principals with their faculties can move—as some already have—ahead of their contemporaries to produce models of excellence to which others may aspire. Energy, commitment, and a faith born of adequate professional knowledge can serve as the springboard for dramatic achievement in education. We owe ourselves and our children nothing less.

References

Berliner, D.; Tikunoff, W.; and Ward, B. *Beginning Teacher Evaluation Study.* San Francisco: Far West Laboratory for Educational Research and Development, 1976.

Brophy, J. "Teacher Behavior and Its Effects." *Journal of Teacher Education* 71 (1979): 733-750.

Coleman, J. S., and others. *Equality of Educational Opportunity.* Washington, D.C.: U.S. Government Printing Office, 1966.

Edmonds, R. "Some Schools Work and More Can." *Social Policy* (March/April 1979): 29-32.

Feuerstein, R., and others. *The Dynamic Assessment of Retarded Performers.* Baltimore: University Park Press, 1979.

Feuerstein, R., and others. *Instrumental Enrichment.* Baltimore: University Park Press, 1980.

Freire, P. *Pedagogy of the Oppressed.* New York: Herder and Herder, 1968.

Fuller, R. *In Search of the IQ Correlation: A Scientific Whodunit.* Stonybrook, N.Y.: Ball-Stick-Bird, Inc., 1977.

Ginsberg, H. *The Myth of the Deprived Child: Poor Children's Intellect and Education.* Englewood Cliffs, N.J.: Prentice-Hall, 1972.

Jensen, A. *Bias in Mental Testing.* New York: Free Press, 1980.

Rosenthal, R., and Jacobson, L. *Pygmalion in the Classroom.* New York: Holt, Rinehart & Winston, 1968.

Snow, R. E. *A Model Teacher Training System.* Stanford, Calif.: Stanford Center for Research and Development in Teaching, 1972.

Stallings, J. A. *Follow-Through Program Classroom Observation Evaluation, 1971-1972.* Menlo Park, Calif.: Stanford Research Institute, 1973.

11.

Leadership for Strengthening Basic Skills Education

William D. Georgiades
and B. Dell Felder

The Principal Makes the Difference

Changing educational practice is much too complex for simplistic explanations, yet one thing seems clear. When a school implements a new
program, or changes an existing one, the principal is often the key to the
success or failure of that effort. As an instructional leader, the principal's
job is to help the people in a school make educational programs work.
There is no program that you can buy or create that will increase basic
skills achievement in a school unless the people who work there want to
make the program work.

Improving basic skills often requires different instructional methods
or new materials. Changing educational practice is intrinsically disruptive.
Change threatens people; it upsets established routines; it takes extra
energy and time; it challenges the status quo.

How do successful principals manage change in their schools? What
leadership styles do they employ? What roles do they play? What administrative behaviors work best? While there is no one answer to these questions, three things are crucial for principals.

First, the principal is the person who must provide the leadership
for improvement. The principal must recognize that a problem exists and
that improvement is necessary. The principal must create a shared concern for improving the situation by involving teachers in deciding what
is to be done and by orchestrating people and resources to accomplish
the task. Indeed, without the commitment and leadership of the principal,
most efforts to improve programs in secondary schools will never get off
the ground. It is the principal who must provide the *energy* for change.

Second, the principal must recognize that he or she will be most
effective when leadership behaviors match staff expectations. In fact, the

127

principal's ability to selectively use a variety of leadership styles to match the situation, the task, and the expectations of subordinates is a key to success. Determining the type of leadership that is appropriate for any given situation is a skill. It involves recognizing the conditions inherent in varying situations and consciously deciding how goals might be best achieved in those circumstances. In order to do this, principals must recognize available options and apply them to varying circumstances.

Third, the principal must play a variety of roles and realize that those roles will change as the process of improving a program evolves. In studying principals who successfully implemented new programs in their schools, one group of researchers found that the successful principal was many things:

. . . he or she was a *believer,* feeling a genuine commitment to the project; an *advocate* who promoted and defended the project before a variety of audiences; a *linker* who connected the project with other parts of the system; a *resources acquirer* who obtained and allocated tangible and intangible resources for the project; an *employer* who hired project staff or assigned teachers to it; a *leader* who supplied initiative, energy, and direction; a *manager* who provided problem-solving assistance and support; a *delegator* who "moved backstage" when teachers assumed leadership; a *supporter* with words of encouragement and acts of assistance; and an *information source* who gave feedback to teachers and project staff.[1]

A Matter of Style

When a principal chooses a leadership style, there is always the question of how much authority and responsibility he or she will give to others. Tannenbaum and Schmidt suggest that there are six leadership styles that fall on a continuum from high authority and responsibility vested in the principal to high authority and responsibility vested in the staff, as shown in Figure 1.[2]

When *telling,* the principal chooses a course of action and tells the staff what they are expected to do. The staff does not participate in decisions. When *selling,* the principal usually makes a decision and then attempts to persuade the staff to accept it. When *testing,* the principal proposes a solution and asks the staff to react to it. When *consulting,* the principal gives the staff a chance to influence a decision from the begin-

---

[1] Spencer H. Wyant, *Of Projects and Principals* (Reston, Va.: Association of Teacher Educators, 1980).

[2] Robert Tannenbaum and Warren H. Schmidt, "How to Choose a Leadership Pattern," Harvard Business Review 51 (May-June 1973).

ning. The principal may present the problem and related information, but the staff is asked to offer solutions. The principal then selects the solutions he or she believes will be most effective. When *delegating,* the principal gives the decision-making responsibility to the staff with or without reserving veto power or modification rights. When *joining,* the principal is an equal participant in the decision making process, and has no more or no less power than other members of the staff.

Figure 1. Continuum of Authority and Responsibility Vested in the Principal and the Staff

Principal maximum Staff minimum					Staff maximum Principal minimum
Telling	Selling	Testing	Consulting	Delegating	Joining

Each of these leadership styles can be effective, and there are other models that provide sound conceptualizations of behaviors to guide administrative action. Two points in particular should be kept in mind. Effective administrators acknowledge their limitations and recognize the roles they do not perform well. Also, it is not a principal's intention that determines whether a particular style will be effective; it is how that style affects other people. In other words, the staff's response and reaction to a principal's actions determine whether the choice of a particular style was a wise one.

The Context

Improvements in educational practice occur in the context of a school setting. That context always has two dimensions—the job to be done, the *task;* and the people involved, the *process.* Both of these dimensions require the principal's attention. Successful principals understand the difference between the two and use appropriate administrative behaviors in both dimensions.

In dealing with the *task* of improving basic skills programs, the most important responsibilities of the principal are: (1) to understand what is being done; (2) to demonstrate commitment to the project and visualize its intended outcomes; (3) to negotiate competing pressures within and outside the school; and (4) to allocate and use resources effectively.

A principal's knowledge of a project is critical to the staff's feeling that they can depend on administrative understanding and support for their work. The principal is not necessarily expected to know everything about the project, or to be an "expert" on every school task. But the staff expects the principal to have sufficient understanding to work effectively with them and to communicate the school's efforts eloquently. When teachers are doing something new, they are taking more risks than they normally would. They expect the principal to understand the demands placed on them, to value their mistakes as well as their failures, and to communicate to others what they are attempting and why they are attempting it.

Principals must demonstrate a strong commitment to basic skills programs in their schools. Nothing kills an improvement effort faster than a staff who believes the principal does not care about the project. Thus the principal's visible commitment is critical to success. Teachers are quick to recognize superficial commitment. Principals must "practice what they preach." They cannot expect teachers to change if they are unwilling to accommodate needed changes in their own roles.

Schools are political. Competition for resources is keen and special interests vie constantly for control. The political implications of any effort to change the school must be understood by the principal, who must competently explain, defend, protect, and run interference for the project. Often, only the principal is in a position to negotiate competing pressures. There are criticisms and misunderstandings whenever a school changes unless the principal provides effective liaison and communication linkages within the school district and into the community.

Resources are the ingredients that improve basic skills programs. They are tangible and intangible; they include money, people, materials, equipment, and influence. The principal is expected to acquire resources and allocate them in ways that assure success. Resource needs for successful project implementation may be as diverse as an "opening" in the school schedule, space in the building, or the use of influence and leadership to obtain regulatory waivers or community and school volunteers.

The other dimension of the school setting that concerns principals is the people who bring about the improvements. The principal who works effectively with people in the school and community employs behaviors that: (1) clarify roles to be performed; (2) encourage involvement and participation; (3) communicate support and personal commitment; and (4) provide staff with feedback that facilitates growth in skills and confidence.

Managing the task (job to be done) and managing the process (dealing with the people involved) simultaneously may seem dichotomous. The principal may feel caught between the management demands of both dimensions. Yet, knowing when to handle the people problems and when to attend to task concerns is one of the most important skills an administrator can develop.

Change threatens some people. In fact, having to depart from established routines and ways of thinking and doing things can create serious psychological trauma. Hall and others found that teachers go through predictable stages of concern in their efforts to create new programs.[3] Initially, teachers may have little concern about becoming involved in a new program, but they begin to seek more information as their awareness of an innovation increases. Personal concerns mount as teachers realize they may become personally involved with an innovation. Questions regarding professional and personal adequacy to meet new demands surface, and status issues emerge. At the point of initial program implementation, teachers' concerns about day-to-day processes and tasks increase. This stage, called management concerns, continues until teachers develop a smooth and routine procedure. In the next stage, teachers' concerns are likely to shift to program consequences for students. Finally, teachers may also experience concerns about collaborating with others and about exploring ways to modify the innovation to increase student achievement.

Hall and his colleagues also found that as people change from one set of educational practices to another, they experience predictable difficulties. Normally, teachers go through several levels of use as an innovation is implemented. From a state of non-use, teachers begin to learn more about a new program and enter an orientation stage and a preparation stage. At the point that implementation begins, teachers are mechanical users; that is, they direct their efforts primarily to managing the day-to-day, short-term demands a new program usually presents. As routine patterns for using the innovation develop, teachers' usage patterns stabilize. Changes in program use proceed from formal or informal evaluation data rather than from attempts to overcome difficulties. Finally, teachers reach the refinement level when program modifications affect both short- and long-term consequences for students.

Knowledge of an individual staff member's "stages of concern" and "levels of use" allows the principal to provide assistance and support when needed. For example, a teacher who is experiencing frustration and difficulties getting something new to work in the classroom does not need a sermon on the long-term benefits of the new program. What that teacher

---

[3] G. E. Hall and S. F. Loucks, "Teacher Concerns as a Basis for Facilitating and Personalizing Staff Development," *Teacher College Record* 80 (1978): 36-53.

needs is someone to illustrate how to make the program work in the classroom.

Managing Programs to Improve Basic Skills

Most programs for educational improvement go through similar cycles or stages in their development. Each cycle requires the principal to play a somewhat different role and to choose administrative behaviors appropriate for varying situations. A simple way of thinking about project cycles is to consider the major phases of a program's growth, as shown in Figure 2.

Figure 2. Phases of Program Growth

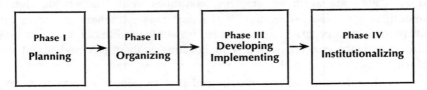

Phase I: Planning

The major activities associated with Phase I, planning, involve (1) developing awareness that change is needed; (2) defining the problem to be solved; (3) assessing the school's readiness for change; (4) identifying and evaluating alternative solutions; and (5) deciding on a course of action.

The principal's commitment is absolutely essential to launching and planning an effort to improve basic skills instruction. He or she is usually in the best position to recognize that change is needed. The principal has access to a wide range of information including student achievement records, observations, and reactions from staff and parents. He or she can also underscore the importance of responding affirmatively to existing needs. It is most appropriate, therefore, that the principal present information about the problem and possible procedures for solving it after gathering faculty ideas. Diagnostic and consulting leadership styles are likely to be effective for this phase.

As awareness of a need for change in the school is established, the principal must involve faculty in deciding what course of action to follow. Those who are expected to implement the change should join the program planning effort as early as possible. Without joint planning, problems may arise later in operating the program according to original intentions. People also like to participate in making decisions that affect them; it generates a feeling of control and contributes to a sense of trust in collaborative relationships.

Schools, like people, vary in their capacity to accommodate change. It is important that the principal take time to assess the school's readiness for change, which can be done by studying existing conditions and asking the following questions:

1. How strongly is the staff committed to the need for change? Do they believe basic skills achievement can be improved?

2. How stable is the staff? Will those who plan the new basic skills programs implement them?

3. Does the faculty work cooperatively? Do they need to develop new collaborative skills?

4. What technical skills will be needed to implement the new program? Does the faculty have those skills? Can they be developed quickly through inservice programs or other means?

5. Does the school climate encourage cooperation and collaborative efforts?

6. Is the faculty willing to take risks? Will they try something new? How do they handle frustration and failure?

During another important aspect of the planning phase, the planners analyze proposed program alternatives to determine their likelihood of success. Each option has a potential impact on the school and its personnel. It is necessary to recognize and understand this impact at the outset. Some programs require major changes in roles and teaching behaviors and are harder to implement successfully than others. Some programs necessitate expensive equipment acquisition or facility modifications. Further, a school can become overloaded with new programs and innovations. As a result, the faculty may be unable to adjust to the many new demands placed on them. When this occurs, efforts to improve education are usually aborted.

During the planning phase of the program, the principal's major roles are as a *leader,* providing the initiative and motivation for addressing the problems; as an *information source,* assisting in the delineation of the problem's parameters and in the identification of possible acceptable solutions; as an *advocate,* expressing commitment to the appropriate solution;

and as a *linker,* uniting the school, the central administration, and the community to ensure support and needed resources.

Phase II: Organizing

In the second phase of the program, organizing, the people and resources needed to implement the program are acquired and organized. Effective leadership styles for this phase involve selling, testing, consulting, and delegating.

Personnel to operate the program will most likely be obtained in one of two ways: if resources are available, new personnel might be hired; otherwise existing staff roles will need to be redefined. When selecting personnel, the principal should seek individuals who have needed technical skills and who display an ability to work effectively with others. They should be highly motivated and committed to the project. In some cases, special interests may need to be protected and represented. Such factors as grade level, department representation, and sex and ethnic differences may need to be considered.

In some schools, it may be difficult to "bring everybody along" in a new effort to improve basic skills instruction. However, it is important that *all* faculty know what is being proposed and how the new program might affect them. While some faculty may never choose to join the new program, they should be encouraged to remain neutral and not actively resist program efforts.

After staff selection and program organization, the principal's key role is to *delegate* appropriate responsibility and authority for program implementation. This may be especially difficult for some principals, particularly if they are authoritative in style or if they had great personal involvement in the program's design. Delegating is not abdicating, however, and the principal should remember that ultimate responsibility and accountability will remain in his or her office. The principal should also carefully examine program management responsibility and consciously decide how much authority to share with the program staff.

Effective delegation of responsibility gives the staff a clear charge. This charge communicates expectations and achieves agreement on roles and outcomes. The principal's charge to the staff states in detail the task to be accomplished, sets deadlines, identifies constraints and non-negotiables (such as policies, regulations, and the like), establishes limits of authority, and announces the principal's personal preferences for program operation. During this phase, the principal's chief roles are as *employer,* selecting and assigning staff; and as *delegator,* setting forth the task to be accomplished.

Phase III: Developing and Implementing

During Phase III, developing and implementing the program, the principal's role usually shifts from leader to manager. Principals generally assume a much less directive role and use more relationship-oriented administrative behaviors. Appropriate leadership styles include delegating and joining.

During this phase, instructional materials are acquired or developed, new teaching methods are tried, staff training is provided, and the program is put "on line." This is the most likely time for unanticipated problems to arise. Procedures won't work as planned, or resources are inadequate, or the program generates critical reactions from parents, students, or the school board. This phase can be especially frustrating for the principal for he or she must patiently allow the staff sufficient latitude to do the job. "Patiently" means taking a back seat even when the "I can do it better by myself" urge becomes strong.

Effective principals remember that their ultimate goal is to remove themselves from the program; that is, to have the staff so fully committed and competent in operating the program that they forget the principal was ever substantially involved in providing initiative and leadership for the effort.

Formal program evaluation should begin during this phase. Information about student achievement and student-teacher satisfaction with the program should be gathered. The principal also should constantly seek information on program staff morale and student and community attitudes toward the new instructional program. Is it receiving "bouquets or brickbats" from the central administration and the community? It is especially important that those who are not directly involved with the program perceive that they are getting their fair share of the principal's attention and the school's resources. The perception that the program provides "special favors" to a select few should be especially avoided.

It is crucial that the principal provide a high degree of support to staff during this phase. Recognizing achievement, working collaboratively to resolve problems, listening, extending empathy, expressing thanks, providing feedback, offering assistance, checking with staff to find out how they are doing and what they are feeling, going to inservice meetings, and attending program staff conferences are ways a principal says "I care; we can make it together for it is important to our school and our students."

During Phase III, the principal's major roles are as *advocate,* selling, protecting, and defending the program; as *linker,* connecting the project to other parts of the school system and the community; and as *resource acquirer,* using skill and influence to obtain and to allocate needed resources.

Phase IV: Institutionalizing

In the final phase of the program cycle, overall success is judged, and decisions on continuation are made. If deemed worthy, the program moves from an experimental form into an institutionalized routine. During this time, the principal assumes consulting, evaluative, and selling styles of leadership.

If accurate data on program outcomes have been systematically collected, and if the principal has taken the temperature of the faculty and students along the way, it would seem fairly simple to determine whether the program merits continuation. It is important, however, that principals include the faculty in deciding whether to retain an experimental program. Two advantages accrue from faculty collaboration: key program modifications may be suggested that could salvage a potentially sound program from the scrapheap; and the staff will likely maintain or even increase their commitment to the program.

If a program merits continuation, it probably has been cost effective. However, resource availability on a long-term basis is an important issue in institutionalization.

During this final phase, the principal's roles are as an *information source,* providing data for continuation decisions; as a *leader,* providing direction for future efforts; as an *advocate,* selling the program if results merit continuation; and as a *resource acquirer,* obtaining long-term commitments for institutionalization.

12.

The Significance of Leadership in Effective School Management

Vincent E. Reed

In a recent interview, a member of the board of education for the District of Columbia Public Schools predicted that the success of a proposed extended volunteer project will largely depend on the dynamics that individual principals can bring to bear as the plan develops. This basic assumption not only reflects the theory that many people hold about the impact of leadership on organizational behavior, but it also underscores the pivotal point from which effective school management revolves.

It is well known that coaches of great athletic teams rarely have the experience of having played every position required in competition; yet through leadership, their teams are synchronized to demonstrate a combination of skills that distinguishes them in the sports arena. By the same token, most managers of a school or school system probably have not actively participated in every operational aspect of the educational structure, but their effective leadership enables them to build units that competently deliver services to students. Thus, the leadership style of the person at the top determines management.

The nature of leadership is varied and complex, and might be more comprehensively explained by one having broader knowledge of the behavioral sciences. Its essence, however, is in motivating people to work willingly, harmoniously, and zealously toward predetermined goals. Specifically, it includes:

- Setting standards and persuading the community, the staff, and the students to agree with and adhere to them
- Motivating the work of the staff by giving meaningful directions
- Enlisting community support in helping to attain goals
- Assisting teachers and administrators to develop more creative approaches to education by improving their individual skills

137

- Encouraging staff members and parents to critically examine activities and programs
- Securing resources for school programs
- Building a sense of pride in the work accomplished and generating enthusiasm for that remaining to be done.

Each of these aspects of leadership brings into focus the importance of interpersonal relationships, thus making it evident that an outstanding leader is a manager, a mover, a manipulator of people. One of the crucial factors of success in contemporary school management involves the effectiveness of principals or superintendents in influencing their communities. Thus, the primary characteristics of the administrative leader include the ability to inspire confidence; to manifest positiveness without being dictatorial; to exemplify fairness; and above all, to convince the public that as the person in charge, he or she has purpose, knows what to do, and understands where educational programs are going and how they will get there.

Moreover, a leader must be able to accept criticism. In fact, a leader should encourage it, not only to gauge the mood and opinions of constituents, but also to provide a sense of direction for school programs. For example, a local Washington, D.C. radio station emphasizes to its listeners its editorial position that the schools should provide training for students in areas of demand by local employers. This position simply highlights a community need that has strong implications for a focus the public schools might make in planning course offerings. It is a healthy way of nudging educators to take a practical and positive step that will be beneficial to students and to business.

Finally, leadership is synonymous with courage—the courage to make decisions, including those that involve controversial or unpleasant issues. It means persisting in a goal even when others say it cannot be done. It means overcoming people's natural inertness and influencing them to move ahead; and it also means the ability to work hard, to demonstrate by example that diligence and effort do lead to success.

Years ago, American school children were presented with what some historians describe as a glorified version of the discovery of this country. They learned that courage, persistence, and hard work brought Christopher Columbus and his apprehensive crew to the unknown shores of a "new" world, and that the decision to "sail on" despite adversity and overwhelming odds changed the course of world history. This story dramatically portrays Columbus as a bold man whose convictions, even in the face of mutiny by his entire crew, motivated him to pursue his goal. Perhaps the details of this episode are magnified to some degree, but the portrait of leadership is real. Men and women who are guided by principles, who give serious thought to the possible consequences of their decisions, and who stand prepared to assume responsibility for their actions possess the qualities that are needed to move organizations forward.

To move ahead, however, a leader must have a vision; that is, a leader must have a long view into the future as well as fresh insight into the facts of the present. A leader must be able to see the difference between what "should be" and what "actually is." The process of carving out a specified destination, determining the best path to take to reach it, and establishing indicators of success along the route are basic steps in program planning, an essential element of effective school management.

This process is used in making the decisions that have the most impact on an organization. For example, it may be used to examine an existing policy on the promotion of students from grade to grade for the purpose of making substantive but positive changes, or it may be used to determine the programmatic thrust when budget reductions are mandated. Both principals and superintendents will find this process highly beneficial in implementing policies mandated by boards of education.

Moreover, the increasing demand for accountability in education requires the strict assessment of a school's service to the public. In the last decade, the American taxpayer has persistently raised questions about the productivity and effectiveness of the nation's public schools. The message is clear that educators must develop specific procedures for measuring and showing proof of getting the job done. This can be accomplished by using the described process of program planning. Schools that use this system can outline where they want to go and how they plan to get there. In addition, an evaluation component, which forms the basis for appraisal, is inherent in the process.

In sum, then, the key factors for success in management are the leader's depth of perception regarding the purposes of education, the leader's ability to systematically plan toward making those purposes realities, and the leader's skill in motivating people to buy into the programmatic thrust. This is the essence of school management.

About the Authors

ARTHUR N. APPLEBEE is Director of the National Study of Secondary School Writing, and Associate Professor, School of Education, Stanford University, Stanford, California.

DON M. BOILEAU is Director of Educational Services, Speech Communication Association, Annandale, Virginia.

B. DELL FELDER is Professor of Curriculum and Instruction, University of Houston, Houston, Texas.

WILLIAM D. GEORGIADES is Dean, College of Education, University of Houston, Houston, Texas.

ASA G. HILLIARD, III, is Fuller E. Callaway Professor of Urban Education, Georgia State University, Athens.

ELAINE LINDHEIM is Director of Test Development, Instructional Objectives Exchange, Culver City, California.

W. JAMES POPHAM is Director of Instructional Objectives Exchange, and Professor, Graduate School of Education, University of California, Los Angeles.

ARNULFO G. RAMIREZ is Associate Professor of Education, State University of New York, Albany.

VINCENT E. REED is Assistant Secretary for Elementary and Secondary Education, United States Department of Education, Washington, D.C.

JANE A. STALLINGS is Director of Stallings Teaching and Learning Institute, Mountain View, California.

B. ROSS TAYLOR is Mathematics Consultant and Supervisor, Minneapolis Public Schools, Minneapolis, Minnesota.

JUDITH THELEN is Coordinator, Graduate Reading Program, Frostburg State College, Frostburg, Maryland.

M. JERRY WEISS is Distinguished Service Professor of Communications, Jersey City State College, Jersey City, New York.

ASCD Publications, Spring 1982

Yearbooks

A New Look at Progressive Education
(610-17812) $8.00
Considered Action for Curriculum Improvement
(610-80186) $9.75
Education for an Open Society
(610-74012) $8.00
Evaluation as Feedback and Guide
(610-17700) $6.50
Feeling, Valuing, and the Art of Growing:
Insights into the Affective
(610-77104) $9.75
Life Skills in School and Society
(610-17786) $5.50
Lifelong Learning—A Human Agenda
(610-79160) $9.75
Perceiving, Behaving, Becoming: A New Focus
for Education (610-17278) $5.00
Perspectives on Curriculum Development
1776-1976 (610-76078) $9.50
Schools in Search of Meaning
(610-75044) $8.50
Staff Development/Organization Development
(610-81232) $9.75
Supervision of Teaching (610-82262) $10.00

Books and Booklets

About Learning Materials (611-78134) $4.50
Action Learning: Student Community Service
Projects (611-74018) $2.50
Adventuring, Mastering, Associating: New
Strategies for Teaching Children
(611-76080) $5.00
Applied Strategies for Curriculum Evaluation
(611-81240) $5.75
Approaches to Individualized Education
(611-80204) $4.75
Bilingual Education for Latinos
(611-78142) $6.75
Classroom-Relevant Research in the Language
Arts (611-78140) $7.50
Clinical Supervision—A State of the Art Review
(611-80194) $3.75
Curriculum Leaders: Improving Their Influence
(611-76084) $4.00
Curriculum Materials 1981 (611-81266) $5.00
Curriculum Theory (611-77112) $7.00
Degrading the Grading Myths: A Primer of
Alternatives to Grades and Marks
(611-76082) $6.00
Developing Basic Skills Programs in
Secondary Schools (611-82264) $5.00
Developmental Supervision: Alternative
Practices for Helping Teachers Improve
Instruction (611-81234) $5.00
Educating English-Speaking Hispanics
(611-80202) $6.50
Effective Instruction (611-80212) $6.50
Elementary School Mathematics: A Guide to
Current Research (611-75056) $5.00
Eliminating Ethnic Bias in Instructional
Materials: Comment and Bibliography
(611-74020) $3.25
Global Studies: Problems and Promises for
Elementary Teachers (611-76086) $4.50
Handbook of Basic Citizenship Competencies
(611-80196) $4.75
Humanistic Education: Objectives and
Assessment (611-78136) $4.75
Learning More About Learning
(611-17310) $2.00

Mathematics Education Research
(611-81238) $6.75
Measuring and Attaining the Goals of Education
(611-80210) $6.50
Middle School in the Making
(611-74024) $5.00
The Middle School We Need
(611-75060) $2.50
Moving Toward Self-Directed Learning
(611-79166) $4.75
Multicultural Education: Commitments, Issues,
and Applications (611-77108) $7.00
Needs Assessment: A Focus for Curriculum
Development (611-75048) $4.00
Observational Methods in the Classroom
(611-17948) $3.50
Open Education: Critique and Assessment
(611-75054) $4.75
Partners: Parents and Schools
(611-79168) $4.75
Professional Supervision for Professional
Teachers (611-75046) $4.50
Reschooling Society: A Conceptual Model
(611-17950) $2.00
The School of the Future—NOW
(611-17920) $3.75
Schools Become Accountable: A PACT
Approach (611-74016) $3.50
The School's Role as Moral Authority
(611-77110) $4.50
Selecting Learning Experiences: Linking
Theory and Practice (611-78138) $4.75
Social Studies for the Evolving Individual
(611-17952) $3.00
Staff Development: Staff Liberation
(611-77106) $6.50
Supervision: Emerging Profession
(611-17796) $5.00
Supervision in a New Key (611-17926) $2.50
Urban Education: The City as a Living
Curriculum (611-80206) $6.50
What Are the Sources of the Curriculum?
(611-17522) $1.50
Vitalizing the High School (611-74026) $3.50
Developmental Characteristics of Children and
Youth (wall chart) (611-75058) $2.00

Discounts on quantity orders of same title to single address: 10-49 copies, 10%; 50 or more copies, 15%. Make checks or money orders payable to ASCD. Orders totaling $20.00 or less must be prepaid. Orders from institutions and businesses must be on official purchase order form. Shipping and handling charges will be added to billed purchase orders. *Please be sure to list the stock number of each publication, shown in parentheses.*

Subscription to *Educational Leadership*—**$18.00 a year. ASCD Membership dues: Regular (subscription [$18] and yearbook)—$38.00 a year; Comprehensive (includes subscription [$18] and yearbook plus other books and booklets distributed during period of membership)—$48.00 a year.**

Order from:

**Association for Supervision and
Curriculum Development
225 North Washington Street
Alexandria, Virginia 22314**